P9-DYD-634

Mom Management

Managing Mom Before Everybody Else

Marilyn, Thanks for your support + encouragement! Take care of the Me in Grand Mommeee!

Tracy Lyn Moland

Tracy Lyn Moland

Foreword by Patricia Cobe and Ellen H. Parlapiano, authors of the Mompreneurs® Books
Introduction by Sandi Richard, author of the *Cooking for the Rushed* series

TGOT
Calgary, Alberta, Canada
www.thegiftoftime.ca

Mom Management, Managing Mom Before Everybody Else. Copyright©
2003 by Tracy Lyn Moland. All rights reserved. No part of this book may be
reproduced in any form or by an electronic or mechanical means including
information storage and retrieval systems without permission in writing from the
publisher, except by a reviewer, who may quote brief passages in a review.
Published by The Gift of Time, Calgary, Alberta, Canada. info@thegiftoftime.ca
First Printing 2002

Printed in Canada.

Visit our Web site at **www.MomManagement.com** for more information.

National Library of Canada Cataloguing in Publication Data

Moland, Tracy Lyn, 1969-
  Mom management : managing mom before everybody else / Tracy Lyn
Moland.

Includes bibliographical references.
ISBN 0-9730704-0-4

1. Mothers. 2. Time management. 3. Family--Time management. I.
Title.
HQ759.M57 2002   640'.43   C2002-911348-2

Although the author and publisher have exhaustively researched all sources to
ensure the accuracy and completeness of the information contained in this book,
we assume no responsibility for errors, inaccuracies, omissions, or any other
inconsistency herein. Any slights against people or organizations are unintentional.
Readers should use their own judgement or consult their health care provider
before starting any exercise program or diet.

**ATTENTION LIBRARIES, WOMENS ORGANIZATIONS,
MOTHERS GROUPS AND RETAILERS:** Quantity discounts are
available on bulk purchases of this book for educational purposes,
fundraising, or gift giving. Specials books, booklets or book exerts can also
be created to fit specific needs. For information, please contact TGOT,
www.thegiftoftime.ca, (403) 226-8798, books@thegiftoftime.ca

Edited by Amanda Ayles, www.AmandaMarks.com
Photographs by Marilyn Gillespie, www.marilyngillespie.com
Layout by Terri Pepin, www.mapleleafsolutions.com

Pat
Thank You for your love and confidence in me.

Courtney-Lyn and Mats
You've made me a Mom Manager
I love you very much

Terri
I don't know how to thank you enough.
This book would not be a reality without you.
You truly are my kindred spirit.

Thank You to all the Mothers, especially my own,
who helped create this book by providing
your insights and suggestions.

Thank you to the team of people whose support and work made this book possible. Thank you for your work, your support and your suggestions. Thank you to my wonderful family, Sandi and Ron Richard, Patricia Cobe, Ellen H. Parlapiano, Jenny Hoops, Amanda Ayles, Patricia Verge, Tim Breithaupt, Jennifer Kirk, Dixie Schmidt, Harwant Johnson, Alice Hoover, Natalie Gomersall, Annette Graf, Diana Leitch, Marilyn Gillespie, Paula Polman, Jim Beckel, Debbie Muir, St. Petersburg Church Moms group, Crossfield Mops and all the Mompreneurs®!

FOREWORD
BY THE MOMPRENEURS®

Most of us embark on the amazing journey of motherhood never realizing how much time day-to-day parenting actually takes. Before children, which one of us could ever imagine going through an entire day without being able to fit in a five-minute shower? Yet every mom with a newborn has spent many unwashed and rumpled hours in her bathrobe, focused entirely on her baby's needs. And who would think that a six-year old's academic, social, and athletic life could be so tightly scheduled, it could leave the average mom with no time to boil pasta for dinner—much less sit down and read the newspaper? We've all been there, too.

Tracy Lyn Moland has also been there. And it's from this firsthand experience that she discovered it was possible - and downright necessary - for every mom to forge an identity apart from her role as mother. What's more, Tracy shows us how we can reclaim our sense of self *and* become better parents in the process. Her secret - using effective management skills to explore dreams, set goals, and organize time and space.

Just seeing the words "time management" on a book can stress out a mom before she even starts reading. Someone who buys a birthday present on the way to the party and wraps it in the car just can't relate to that kind of "business speak!" But

Mom Management is calming and non-threatening from the very first page. It's almost as if Tracy is holding your hand as she takes you on a journey of self-discovery. Baby step by baby step, you can follow along at your own pace, as she gently guides you in creating a Life Map, balancing your many roles, and finding reservoirs of time you never thought existed. Through personalized activities and practical advice, the book motivates and encourages moms to sneak in and schedule the "me" time they so desperately need.

Reading is one of those luxuries that time-starved mothers often postpone or do without. But make the time to read *Mom Management*—you'll be glad you did.

Patricia Cobe and Ellen H. Parlapiano

Patricia Cobe and Ellen H. Parlapiano, are the authors of Mompreneurs®: A Mother's Practical Step-by-Step Guide to Work-at-Home Success (Perigee, 2002) and Mompreneurs® Online: Using the Internet to Build Work@Home Success (Perigee, 2001). Visit them at http://www.mompreneursonline.com

Table of Contents

INTRODUCTION
BY SANDI RICHARD

In my own personal journey, people would ask me, "What do you do for a living?" "Well, I'm a...well, I'm a ...". I was always trying to figure out exactly *who* I was.

I was a publisher, I guess. After all, I had two books that were best sellers many times over.

Or was I a cook? After all, my specialty is meal planning.

But, then again, was I in the business of *Helping People*? When I leave someone with a skill and they tell me it has changed their life for the better, it's a real high for me.

But of all the things I do, I feel most rewarded when I see myself as a great parent. (Though, at this point in my life, with teen-aged children, I can attest I'm in constant review of my parenting skills!). Of all the things I do, I think I do that the best.

So, I'm always left feeling confused after being asked that question. It shoots me off into a private, self- evaluation of: "*What am I **really** here for?*"

When I read *Mom Management*, I finally understood and embraced my many purposes. For the first time, everything made sense! Tracy Lyn has a unique approach through shoes (yes, shoes!), a life map, a collage and many other exercises that force you to look at what is really important to YOU!!! Somewhere along the way, I had forgotten about *ME!*

i

I suggest you plunk yourself down on the sofa, get a nice cup of tea and enjoy the ride! I guarantee this will be a journey you'll never forget, for the rest of **YOUR** life!!!!

Sandi Richard

Sandi Richard is a meal-planning expert and author of the best-selling cookbooks *Life's On Fire-Cooking for the Rushed* and *Getting' Ya Through the Summer.* Her third book, *The Healthy Family,* has just been released.

Visit www.CookingfortheRushed.com for more information.

MOM MANAGEMENT...

For me, *Mom Management* holds a number of meanings, with *Managing Mom Before Everybody Else* being most important. I have always felt that being a Mom is a lot like being a manager. The skills we use to run our homes are very similar to skills used to run a business.

Regardless of our individual circumstances, we share a common bond - that of being a Mother. Being a Mom is an incredible experience but it is also very consuming. We have all experienced an incredible change from our pre-mother lives. Most of these changes are very positive but one that we all have trouble dealing with is a loss of our sense of self. At some point, we realize that we have let being a Mom become our entire identity. When my children were two and four years old, I realized that Tracy Lyn was missing. In tears, I realized I had lost my sense of self. In looking for myself, I decided to try doing a triathlon, thus setting one goal. Wow! The focus of that one goal, one thing just for me, re-established my sense of self. That initial goal led to five more triathlons, becoming an entrepreneur, a professional speaker, and now an author. During the long process of finding my true self again, I also became a better Mother.

As I realized, being a Mom is not *who* we are, but rather one of the many other roles that we fill in our lives. The term Mom Management and this book were created as reminders that the Me in Mommeee still exists, and needs to be nurtured. Flying provides us with the perfect analogy. At the beginning of each flight, we are told that, "If flying with children, make sure to secure your own oxygen mask first and then secure theirs." As a Mom, we need to take care of ourselves first so that we can better meet the needs of our families. Rather than put ourselves second we need to secure our oxygen masks first.

When we truly care for ourselves, it becomes possible to care far more profoundly about other people. The more alert and sensitive we are to our own needs, the more loving and generous we can be toward others. Eda LeShan

Knowing we need to care for ourselves and doing it are very different things. As Moms, we feel that we are being selfish if we take the extra time to pay better attention to our own needs. This book reveals to everyone that it is not selfishness but an absolute necessity for Moms to be cared for. By providing a variety of ideas, suggestions and tools, Moms have the chance to learn to manage themselves!

A jug fills drop by drop. Buddha

Enjoy the book, do the activities, allow yourself to dream, allow yourself to be, and do what is right for you. Do it over a month or over a year. Determine where you are in life and what you need. At different stages of the journey of motherhood, we experience different demands. A mother of a new baby is experiencing such a learning curve that many of these suggestions seem impossible. Sleep is likely the ultimate dream!

As we move into different stages of motherhood, the demands on our time and energy will vary. This book is intended to be based upon you and your current needs. If an example or suggestion doesn't feel right for you, let it pass you by. Look at your lifestyle, your personality and let your instincts guide you through the exercises.

WHAT TO EXPECT

In this book, I share with you the journey of *Mom Management*. During this journey, we will look at our lives - where we are and where we want to be. We will cover the power of dreaming and goal setting. We will learn to balance the roles we play in life. We will look at how we are wasting time and then how to better use this time for ourselves. We will make sure we are taking care of ourselves. Finally, we will end with a look at two of the skills the career of mothering requires – managing our time and being organized.

Let's begin the journey!

Friendship with oneself is all-important, because without it one cannot be a friend with anyone else in the world. Eleanor Roosevelt

---

HOW TO USE THIS BOOK

There are many activities and worksheets throughout this book. They are tools to help you personalize your Mom Management journey. However, feel free to skip over some or all of the activities during your first read through. As you start applying the ideas to your life or find more *Me Time,* go back and complete the activities. You can easily pick and choose the ones you feel will most benefit you at this time.

This book is written for busy Mothers so only do what is right and makes sense for you. My goal for each mother that reads this book is that you find at least one idea that works for you. You may find yourself re-doing some activities many times and never doing others. You may prefer just to read the book and do the activities in your head or you may want to work on one chapter a month.

As you move through the book, either bookmark activities or use the Activity Worksheet on page 168 to help you keep track of the activities you have done, need to do or would like to re-do.

Reach for the Stars
Dreaming

Reach for the stars because if you should happen to miss, you'll still be among them. Anonymous

DREAMING

The power of a dream - do you remember where your dreams took you as a child? I was a princess, I was a fairy, I was Barbie, I was Olivia Newton-John in *Grease*, I was a pageant contestant, I was an Olympic medallist, I had a castle, I travelled, I had a dolphin, I was the character in my favourite books, I was a detective, I was rich, I was famous, and the list went on. I was one of the lucky ones; I was always encouraged to dream. Yet, somewhere along the way, dreaming started to diminish and the real world took over. Whether told to stop dreaming, to pay attention and focus on the real world, or by nature's course, many people stopped dreaming for good. My own dreams started to fade to the background of my busy schedule. I stopped playing make believe. I stopped pretending I was a famous movie star.

I stopped believing that I could do or be anything I wanted to be. Up until my second year of university, I had complete confidence in myself. I got every job I sought. I knew what I wanted and made sure I got it. Then something happened – was it real life? I started to question myself, "Oh I won't get that job, why bother applying."

Second Guessing

We all went through this phase. We started to second-guess ourselves and our decisions. We stopped listening to our intuition and started listening to others. We did what we thought we should do, not what we wanted to do.

Dreams are the future. They are amazing and they are powerful. As in the quote above; "Reach for the stars – dream and if you should happen to miss, you'll still be among them." I may not be Nancy Drew but I am an author. I may not be a real princess but my children think I am! You may not become Olivia Newton-John but you could be Sandy in a local play.

The dreams of an adult are usually a little different than the dreams of a child but they are still important. I did not dream of being a professional speaker as a child but in my early twenties I saw myself on stage, as a speaker. For some strange reason, I have always dreamed of going to a conference in

Florida… and guess what? That dream came true – twice. Now I dream of speaking at a conference in Florida! I still dream of having a dolphin, but as I look out at the snow around me, I figure that isn't possible - but I will swim with dolphins sometime in my life.

Never give up on your childhood dreams; adulthood affords the opportunity to realize them. Nancy Masco

---

Wow! What a statement! I found this quote while wandering through a beautiful store in the mountains. Its words rang true for me. As children, we can only dream the dreams. As adults, we possess the abilities to bring our dreams to life.

Friends of my family, a couple in their 60s, recently purchased the house of their dreams. It is a huge house, with more room than the two of them need but now that the children have left home, they have the resources for it. When we are camping with the entire family and dog in a tent trailer, invariably there is always a couple alone in a huge motor home beside us. As adults we have the resources, knowledge, beliefs, and possibly, the money and the time (or we know how to find them) to make our dreams of youth come true.

When we stop dreaming, the paths to our dreams will pass us by. If we don't remember or acknowledge what our dreams are, we won't realize when we have the knowledge or

3

opportunity to make them a reality. We won't even notice the advertisement looking for people to be in the play *Grease!* We may miss the opportunity to visit the castles in France or to seize that perfect job.

Open the Door

The first step to getting the things that you want out of life: Decide what you want. Ben Stein

---

I want you to open the door to your dreams. The following activity is your doorknob. It gives you a chance to *BE*, a chance to look back and a chance to look forward.

Never look at the doors closing behind you or you'll miss the ones opening ahead. Cyril Magnin

---

WHAT ARE YOUR DREAMS?
<u>Activity</u>

1. SET A TIMER FOR **FIVE** MINUTES AND LIST ALL THE DREAMS you've ever had – they can be big or small, realistic or unrealistic, anything you think you might want to do, or anything that interests you. This

isn't the time to decide IF you would actually do the things on your list, just write all your thoughts down. Write for the entire time. If you run out of ideas, try to expand on the ones you have. For example, rather than just write travel; choose destinations.

What do you want **TO DO? TO BE? TO HAVE? TO LEARN?** Where do you want **TO GO?**

---

2. TAKE **FIVE** MORE MINUTES AND LOOK OVER YOUR DREAMS. Think about these questions and your current life as you go through your dreams again.

Mom Management

Are you living your life on hold? Are you waiting until - your children are older, you are slimmer, you have more money - to follow your dreams? Are you enjoying the life you are leading? What if you had a limited amount of time left in life and had to choose the dreams that were most important to you? What things jump out at you? The key to this activity is your perspective – it is not about sentimentality but about priorities. Of course, you would put your family and relationships first – but would you keep your job? Would you spend more time with your family? Would you take the time to re-kindle some friendships? What dreams would you choose?

With these questions in mind, **LIST** at least **EIGHT** things that you would most like to accomplish in your lifetime?

1.

2.

3.

4.

Pay off debt

5.

6.

7.

8.

3. NOW COMPARE THE TWO LISTS AND ANSWER
   THESE QUESTIONS:

   What is the difference between them?

   What dreams made the second list?

4. COMPARE YOUR SECOND LIST TO YOUR CURRENT LIFE.

Are they drastically different?

What aren't you doing that you could be doing?

Many of us spend half our time wishing for things we could have if we didn't spend half our time wishing. Alexander Woollcott

---

Over the last few years I have begun to live the life of my dreams, I am caring for myself, I have a strong family, and I am doing the work that I love. If I found out I only had one year of life left, the changes I would make are just minor things. I would swim with dolphins, I would stay in an all-inclusive hotel on a warm beach where I could snorkel for hours, and I would spend two weeks at a hotel in the Disneyworld Resort with my family.

If your dreams are very different from your current life and they include more than things, you need to think about them and ask yourself, "Why?" Do you have to be working at a job you dislike? Could your apply your skills to another career? Do you have to have your children in daycare all the time or could you cut some corners and work three days a week? Is it time for you to re-enter the working world? Could you put your children in child care one or two days a week so you can take that course you've always wanted to take? Can you start with one small change and slowly make the changes necessary for you to live your dreams? Do you have the necessary items to bring your dreams to life - the money, the time, or the resources?

What Changes Would You Make Right Now?

There is a time for everything,
And a season for every activity under the sun. Ecclesiastes 3:1
Yes but they are not the same time. Sara Ban Breathnach

5. PRIORITIZE YOUR DREAMS. You can do most everything you want to in life but you cannot do everything at the same time. Go back through the lists and put a star beside the dreams that mean the most to you right now.

6. PICK YOUR TOP FIVE DREAMS. Look at the dreams that you have marked with stars and pick the

top three to five that you want to start incorporating into your life.

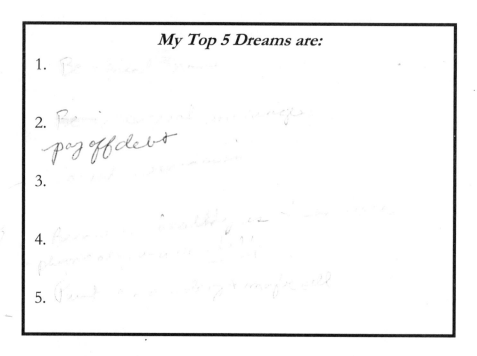

***This is an exercise that you want to re-do every six months to a year. Circumstances can change. As noted above, included on my list of things I would do if I had just one year left, was a trip to an all-inclusive hotel on a beach. When I needed a break from writing my book, guess what trip I took?

In this exercise, we need to be realistic about our current situation. Life is about giving and taking. We may need to schedule some of our dreams around others in our lives. Some things just cannot be done when we have a baby at home or our teens need us around for parental support and guidance. However, many Moms decide to put all their dreams on hold.

There is at least one dream on each of our lists that we can start doing right now. The key to taking care of ME is not to forget about our needs and to incorporate some of our dreams into our lives.

I learned this, at least, by my experiment: that if one advances confidently in the direction of one's dream, and endeavours to live the life which one has imagined, one will meet with a success unexpected in common hours. Henry David Thoreau

---

Be open to your dreams. Be open to what you want for yourself, your family, your relationships, your career and your life. Allow yourself to dream and when you think of new dreams add them to your list.

Dreaming is just the first step. The next step is to act on these dreams. You need to start to *DO* something to make these dreams happen. In the next chapter you will learn the steps you must take to make your dreams become your reality!

COLLAGING

Visual Dreaming

Maybe you aren't sure what your dreams are! Have you forgotten them? Stop your thinking and let your heart take over. Create a collage as a representation of you.

Supplies:MagazinesCataloguesFlyers
ScissorsGlue/tapePaper
Instructions:

1. Flip through magazines and cut out any words, pictures, or sayings that jump out at you.

2. Glue these onto your paper in a way that appeals to you. It can be random or planned.

3. Don't look for things or think about what you are cutting out. Just go with feelings.

4. Add to it continually.

KEY- Put your collage where you will see it every day and take a few minutes just to look at it. Your brain is very powerful. By looking at collages daily, it interprets and internalizes the message and starts to take action. It starts to look for the opportunities to bring the collage to life!

Make this a Family Activity – Teach your children to dream and set goals. We have done it. The children think it is great fun and my husband has learned the power of it! Since creating his first collage six months ago, a number of his dreams have become a reality.

Now that you have identified your dreams – you will be amazed at the opportunities that will appear around you. The steps to your dreams have been there all along but until you realize you are looking for them, they passed you by!

Just like when you were pregnant and noticed pregnant women and babies all over the place; you will now start to see the opportunities for your dreams everywhere.

I skate to where the puck is going to be, not where it is at.
Wayne Gretzky

Dreams of Moms

To raise my children with values that will prepare them for their own futures. *Mom*

To do an Ironman. *Lorry*

Finding time to be fulfilled while still having time for my family. *Christine*

Would love to own a business. *Mom*

To be financially stable. *Adrianna*

To travel the world. *Mom*

Reach a financial level where my spouse can be home more. *Lori*

I want to pursue a career in teaching. *Aubyn*

To continue to grow, not only individually, but also as a partner and a parent. *Lori*

For my business to become an important gift to the community and be a financial success. *Deb*

To finish my bachelor's degree. *Maureen*

To pay off the mortgage. *Ellen*

To be able to stay at home with my children. *Mom*

To finish my doctorate. *Mom*

Take Action
Realizing Your Dreams

The secret of getting ahead is getting started. Sally Berger

THE FIRST STEPS

We've completed the first step – we've started dreaming again. Unfortunately, dreaming isn't doing. Once we have identified our dreams, we must figure out what we can DO to make them come true. DO is the key word.

We need to *DO* something everyday that leads us towards our dreams. I know this statement sounds overwhelming but it is not as hard to accomplish, as it may seem.

When I decided to work towards my dream of doing an Olympic distance triathlon, I did something almost every day that led me to my dream. I took a triathlon training class two days a week. On other days, I would go for a run on my treadmill while the children played, or I would take a swim during their lessons. I would do my stretching while watching TV. And on the days that I didn't train, I fit in activities that led to my other dreams. We should be working towards a few different, non-conflicting dreams at the same time. Doing

15

something to further our dreams may mean doing different things everyday. As I wrote this book, I made sure that it didn't overwhelm my life, and I nurtured my dream of building a strong family unit by spending quality time with them. Rather than writing on the hot summer days, we took advantage of them to do fun family activities.

Enjoy the Journey

It is good to have an end to journey towards; but it is the journey that matters in the end. Ursula LeGuin

The actions we take and the activities we do, not only move us toward our dreams, but also are part of the dream. These activities are as important as the actual realization of the dream itself. While some of the activities may be challenging or difficult, we need to decide to enjoy the journey. Think of a trip – a big part of the excitement is the anticipation! For weeks we are planning the trip - planning what to take, what we will do there, how we will get there and all the while making sure to tell everyone about it. And for weeks after we are telling stories about our adventures, showing our pictures, and cherishing our memories.

Success is never a destination — it's a journey. Satenig St. Marie

There is much more to a dream than the dream itself. Usually the dream represents a feeling we may be looking for or one we have not fully realized. There is a reason we want a bigger house, to feel fit or to travel more.

When planning my trip to Mexico, it wasn't just the desire to see it or swim in the ocean that inspired my plans. It was a need for a few days of full relaxation. I was looking to be free from ringing phones, writing deadlines, cold weather and my dear children demanding attention.

Another example is money - it is not the money itself that people want, but rather what it may bring them. If we were each given a large sum of money, we would have very different uses for it. Some of us are looking for comfort in our current lifestyle. Others want to be confident that the future is secure. Some would help others in need and some of us would use it for fun.

What feelings will your dreams bring you?

TURNING DREAMS INTO ACTIVITIES

So what can we do to realize our dreams? If we dream without taking action, it is impossible for anything to happen. We must first identify two basic elements of our dreams, the WHY and the HOW!

17

Identifying Why

Why do we want to do or have something? Why do we want to be something? Sometimes when we know the why or what we are looking for, we realize we already have it. Or we see a way to adjust something in our lives to get that feeling. The why will vary — wanting a new car may be a need for safety or a longing for a bigger family, money may provide security or a chance to relax, a bigger home may provide peace and quiet, wanting to be fit may represent an unhappiness with our body, and sometimes the why may be *just because*. As I mentioned above my dream for a trip was to fulfill my need to relax. Yes, I could do that anywhere, but the ocean was a big part of that dream!

We need to think through our whys and be careful we aren't looking for things to replace feelings. Finally, we need to make sure that the activities we choose to do are part of the dream and part of the journey.

The people who get on in this world are the people who get up and look for the circumstances they want, and, if they can't find them, make them. George Bernard Shaw

Identifying How

The second step is listing as many activities that relate to your dream as possible. They can be the obvious or the extreme. The key is to list everything that pops into your head and heart. This is only a writing activity. It is not a time to judge, evaluate, analyze, or reflect on the activities. For the time being this exercise is not about you. It is just about all the possible activities that could be done to achieve your dream. To keep it objective, you can do this with a friend – brainstorm together. You are not committing yourself to doing these activities. You are not making any decisions. As Alan Lakein suggests in his book, *How to Get Control of Your Time and Your Life,* "in listing activities, be as imaginative as possible. Quickly write down as many ideas as you can- it's a good way to get creative juices flowing. Trying for quantity and speed will allow your intuition to operate."

The way to acquire enthusiasm is to believe in what you are doing, and in yourself, and in something definite accomplished. Enthusiasm will follow as day follows the night. Dale Carnegie

---

BEGIN THE JOURNEY

Record the Five Dreams you've chosen to focus on from Chapter One – page 10. Take a few minutes and see if you can determine a why for each dream.

My Top 5 Dreams are:

1.

Why? *So that a great ... who ... hue*

2.

Why?

3.

Why? *to believe*

4. *pay off debt*

Why? *more $ for future & things I need & want, + security*

5.

Why?

If you have built castles in the air, your work need not be lost; that is where they should be. Now put the foundations under them. Henry David Thoreau

Activity

Start with just one of these dreams and CREATE an Activity Storm.

1. Spend **FIVE** UNINTERRUPTED MINUTES WRITING DOWN as many activities as you can that relate to this dream. DO NOT stop writing. If you run out of ideas, try to expand on ones you already have written.

For example:

Read a book — Expand to one on parenting, on organization, on time management, on crafts, on decorating, on travelling, on fitness, novels or magazines

Take a Class — types of classes, local schools, Internet, correspondence, art, music, computer, massage

DO activity storms for at least three of your dreams!

Mom Management

Dream:

Activities:

Dream:

Activities:

Dream:

Activities:

Dream:

Activities:

Dream:

Activities:

> *** Just like when you were dreaming, you need to write down *everything* you think of. Don't let judgement get in the way. Don't limit yourself to how you feel now. I remember thinking in university that I could never write a book; I could barely write a paper on the psychology of education. Opportunities and times change. You change! Don't limit yourself.

Sample Activity Storm

Dream: Increase Fitness Level

Activities:walk to work; walk to store; join fitness centre with childcare; skate with kids; bike with family; trade childcare with neighbours; get up early; join a fitness class; buy a fitness video; garden; swim; set a goal of a running race; buy a treadmill or exercise bike; ski as a family; walk the dog; park farther from the door; take the stairs; run around after your kids; exercise at lunch time; use a running stroller; do sit ups and push ups before getting dressed; use the stairs; use a personal trainer; use a yoga tape.

Dream: Further my Education

Activities:research schools in area; start with one night class; attend school part time; take correspondence courses; and take Internet courses

Dream: To Save Money

Activities: Cut out one bought coffee a day; trade childcare with a friend; get a part time job; ask for a raise; cancel unread magazine subscriptions you don't read; use the library; eat at home; use a grocery list and a meal plan; barter services; buy used items; buy in bulk.

2. PRIORITIZE EACH LIST:

- PUT A STAR beside all the things that you think you would like to do or try
- CIRCLE THREE activities that you will begin to incorporate into your life immediately

*Depending on the commitment level of the activities you have chosen, you may want to only concentrate on two or three dreams for now.

Three Activities I will start to do now:

1.

2.

3.

Do not let what you cannot do interfere with what you can do. John Wooden

Three Activities I will start in the next few months:

1.

2.

3.

The next step will be to use these activities to create your **Life Map**. Think of your life as a journey with your dreams being your destination. These activities comprise your schedule or itinerary. Your goals bring it all together in a map.

Know what you want to do, hold the thought firmly, and do every day what should be done, and every sunset will see you that much nearer the goal. Elbert Hubbard

---

Create Your Life Map

3

Goal Setting

A good plan is like a road map: it shows the final destination and usually the best way to get there. H. Stanley Judd

---

GOALS

I used to shudder whenever I heard the word goals. Yes, I heard that they worked, but they seemed so hard to do! Goals were something I didn't want to do. I somehow associated them with negative things, restrictive things, and daunting things. I was so wrong! I didn't understand the power of setting goals. For years, I didn't set them and guess what? Nothing happened. I would think of things I wanted but I wouldn't commit to working towards getting them.

What I failed to realize early on was something that I will again touch on later in this chapter – the journey of life is so much better if we know where we want to go and have a **Life Map** to take us there. I had no idea I needed a **Life Map**, and more importantly, I didn't know that this **Life Map** must consist of the one thing I dreaded – goals. Here is how my *Life Map* evolved.

PRE-DETERMINED GOALS

Although we may not realize it, we have been working towards goals since we were children. Many of these goals were pre-determined. Starting when we were in school our teachers directed us. Our schedules were determined, we knew when we had tests coming up, and we knew what assignments we had to do. When we started to look to the future, we made goals but called them decisions. Do I want to attend post secondary school or not? Do I want to live at home or in residence? Do I want to be a doctor or a hairdresser?

The next steps may have included finding a job and starting our new, adult lives. We may have been looking for an apartment, getting to know a new city, or looking for our life partner (a huge goal in itself). Even in adulthood, life continues to present us with these pre-determined goals.

My Pre-Determined Goals

After finishing university, I met Pat, my future husband, and started my career as a teacher. Within a few years, we decided to get married.

A job promotion took us to another city where after getting married we bought a house, got a puppy, and then we began to consider starting our family.

As we all know, once we start a family, the string of pre-determined goals continues – this time we are following the guidelines of motherhood.

What pre-determined goals are guiding your life right now?

A wedding is an incredible example of goal setting. With the date of the wedding being the long-term goal. There are a number of smaller steps, short-term goals that must be accomplished before we can walk down the aisle!

Self-Imposed Goals

Once I became a Mother, I generally followed these guidelines of motherhood, although I did set a few self-imposed goals. In the fall of 1998, we found ourselves somewhat strapped financially. I also got the notion that we, as a family, needed to go to Disneyworld. My husband thought I was nuts. Still, I wrote the goal down and thought of it often.

Immediately, I started to see opportunities to save money and in May of 1999 we went to Disneyworld - a trip completely paid for by cash! Imagine what might have happened if I had set more goals?

I found myself with another inadvertent set of goals in early 2000. It was my Father's 60th birthday that year and his wife's 50th. My siblings and I decided it was time for a party – thus a new goal was set. Planning the party was like planning a wedding!

No Goals

A few weeks after the party something strange started to happen. I found myself crying at the weirdest times. I was feeling very confused and not sure what was going on. As I looked at my life, I thought I was very happy. I had a wonderful husband, wonderful children, a great home, and a supportive network of friends and family. Pat came home one Friday to find me in tears, yet again. We talked, trying to figure out why I was feeling this way. I knew I needed a change but wasn't sure what that change would be. All I wanted to do was hop on a plane and spend time alone - some time for me to reflect, think and just be. That option just wasn't viable, so I continued on, wondering and thinking.

A New Goal

During that time, I noticed my husband's entry form for an upcoming triathlon. As I read it over, I felt that it was something I needed to do. I went to the local pool to make sure I could swim the distance and being successful, I submitted my application. I then found myself with six weeks in which to prepare to successfully complete a triathlon. With this new focus, I got on with my life. I forgot about crying and my problems. I had a focus, and although I didn't physically write it down, I had a goal. I had a triathlon to complete. I started to train; I swam, I biked, and I ran.

On race day, I got up early and with a very jittery stomach headed out to the race. I was scared and I was excited at the same time. Once I got in the water, I loved it and had a wonderful day. I made a few mistakes but I did the entire race and I felt proud of myself. I felt good again.

I then decided I wanted to do the Olympic distance triathlon, and thus, a new goal was set.

We need a destination for our Journey

I look back now and realize I had let my life fall onto a course with no direction or destination. I had no self-imposed goals, only pre-determined ones. However, I had reached a point in life where the number of pre-determined goals started to decrease. The ones left were less about me and more about my children.

I no longer could direct myself through my journey, because I didn't know where I was going. Once the birthday party was over, I was left with no self-imposed goals to pursue. I had achieved previous goals, and had not set new ones. All it took to get back on track was to find new goals to set.

Once the first was set - the triathlon, I had a focus and I was able to move on. I was then in a state of mind to look to the future and set more goals. I booked my trip alone – it may have been a few months later but I hopped on that plane like I knew I needed to do! I went to Bermuda to visit my brother and relax on the beach.

I started to set goals regularly and as I achieved those goals, I saw positive changes in my life. I began to dream again, taking the time to take care of Tracy Lyn, as well as, my family.

Success

Now after a few years of planned, conscientious goal setting, my life is becoming the life of my dreams! I am a successful entrepreneur, professional speaker and an author. My relationships with my family are stronger than ever and I am in excellent shape. By taking care of myself I have been able to take much better care of my family. I will never allow myself to live without goals again. The journey of life is so much better if you know where you want to go and have a map to take you there.

Activity

Am I setting self-imposed goals, following pre-determined goals or am I at a point in my life where I have NO goals at all?

The Power of Goal Setting

People realize at different ages of their lives the true power of self-imposed goals. Athletes are a perfect example. Simon Whitfield, winner of the first ever gold medal in an Olympic triathlon, visualized himself winning gold long before it was even an Olympic sport. He has a training log he kept from the mid-nineties, and written in it every day is, "I will be an Olympic Gold Medallist."

CREATE YOUR LIFE MAP

Now that we have determined our dreams, brought them back to the surface of our thoughts and come up with activities that we can do to achieve these dreams, we need to take action. I have referred to dreams as a destination and activities as the itinerary. It is now time to put these together and create our action plan – the *Life Map* of our dreams.

Life Map

Road maps are used to determine where we need to go when travelling. We use them to decide which route to take, which direction to go, how long the trip will take, and to determine what to expect along the way.

A *Life Map* is very similar. We use it to map out the route we want our life to take, the direction we want it to go in, to see how long each journey may take, and to determine what else we can expect to encounter along the way.

A road map helps us to stay on course on our trip. A *Life Map* helps us to stay on course in our life. We also need to remember both are not static. When travelling we may come across a detour and need to alter our plans. We may also encounter something new we would like to check out or we may want to park the car and stay somewhere for an extended period of time. Once in a while we may even turn around and go back to the beginning. All of these examples can also apply to your *Life Map*.

Goals give you more than a reason to get up in the morning; they are an incentive to keep you going all day. Goals tend to tap the deeper resources and draw the best out of life. Harvey Mackay

---

TYPES OF GOALS

Goals are set at many different levels. A long-term goal can be very overwhelming so we break it into a number of smaller goals. As we achieve these goals, we can see the progress we are making and the dream is less daunting. Not all goals require you to complete all levels nor do they all come from your dreams. My dishwasher is slowly fading and while it isn't my life long dream to have a new dishwasher, at some point soon I may have to make a short-term goal to start saving for one. A To Do List is actually a short list of several immediate goals with some stemming from your dreams and others from life maintenance items.

Goals should be written down, but it is better to think about and commit to a mental goal than not to have any at all.

Long-Term Goals

A long-term goal is our final destination. It usually takes awhile to complete and needs to be broken into smaller, achievable goals. Once this goal is accomplished, this journey is complete. It is usually one of our dreams.

Intermediate Goals

Intermediate goals are either the pieces that need to be completed to achieve our long-term goals or goals that are in the distance but not as large as the long-term goals. These goals are achieved in a shorter time period.

Short-Term Goals

Short-term goals are accomplished fairly quickly —within one week to one month.

Immediate Goals

Immediate goals are the things we do daily that will lead us to our long-term goals. They are also some of the life maintenance items we just have to get done.

GOAL EVALUATION

From time-to-time we need to re-evaluate our goals. As we progress from our intermediate goals into our short-term goals we need to make sure that we are still on track. We may find that some of the activities we are doing don't actually lead to our long-term goals, or we may find different options. We may find that we don't like something once we try it. Maybe as we are trying to get fit we realize we don't enjoy running. We can still achieve this goal by switching to swimming or yoga. Beware; it is easy to give up when you hit a rough spot or because things aren't going quite right. Goal setting is always rewarding but not always easy.

You must have long-range goals to keep you from being frustrated by short-range failures. Charles C. Noble

If we genuinely find that we just don't like an activity, we may need to change directions. There are many different roads on a road map that we can take to arrive at our destination. Sometimes there will be detours. This is also true of our **Life Map**.

While my goal of running a successful business hasn't changed, the focus of my business has. A detour on my **Life Map** took me from running a successful errand service business to being an author and a speaker. I have removed, added and altered my goals many times. Evaluate your goals every few months.

Getting to our destination does not require perfection; it simply requires a clear picture of where we're going and a willingness to change course as often as it takes to get there.
G. Lynne Snead and Joyce Wycoff

Overlapping Goals

We need to have a variety of goals at the same time. Not all of these goals will be based upon our dreams. We may be saving money for a new car, improving our fitness level, increasing our family time, or simply getting the house cleaned.

As Diana, mother of two and illustrator of *Quillan and Me*, "When we achieve a goal we need to make sure we have another goal started or ready to go so we don't find ourselves lost."

One of the things I like best about travelling without my children is that I don't experience the usual let down at the end of a trip. Rather than being sad that the trip is over, I am excited to get home to my family.

As you come close to the completion of a goal, always be prepared with the answer to this question, "What's next?"

Goal Setting Examples

Using two of the more common dreams of the Moms surveyed – Finding More Time for Me and Getting Fit - see how **Life Maps** are created. Note that they include both the goal and the completion date.

Long-Term Goal
- Finding More Time for Me

- I would like to combine my dream of increasing my fitness level with my dream of having more Me Time by running a 10km race - six months

Intermediate Goals

- I would like to have one hour to myself three times a week – six months.
- I will run/walk a 5km race - three months

Short-Term Goals

- Research running clubs, programs and events – one week
- I will start running/walking 20 minutes three times a week – immediately

Immediate Goals

- Today I will walk for 20 minutes when the kids are at school (or on my lunch break, or I will get up early to walk)

By recording your goals and dreams on paper, you set in motion the process of becoming the person you most want to be. Mark Victor Hansen

---

S.M.A.R.T. Goal Setting

If we can set S.M.A.R.T. goals, we will have a much better chance of realizing them!

S- Specific

You are more likely to accomplish a specific goal than a general one. Make sure your goal includes the five Ws and one H - Who, what, where, when, why, and how.

M- Measurable

How can you know if you have achieved your goal if you can't measure it? Your idea of being financially free may be different than my idea. Include definite numbers, time frames, or occasions to measure your goal. Run 10 km, increase take home pay by $200.00 per month, make two new friends, etc.

A – Achievable

Setting goals is a step-by-step process. Often what seems out of reach today moves into reach tomorrow. Break a large goal into small but attainable goals. If your dream is to run a marathon, start with a goal of a five km race.

R – Rewarding

Most goals come with a reward at the end. Sometimes it is a tangible item like a trip or a new car; other times it is a feeling of pride and success. Remind yourself of the reward of this goal to keep you going if things get difficult. Look at pictures for your trip to Mexico when saving money frustrates you or think about how you will feel when you are in shape.

T – Time

You must have a deadline for your goals. It is okay to change this along the way but if you don't have a deadline you have no motivation to start or keep going.

Deadlines stop our procrastination; they get our adrenaline pumping; they motivate us. Rita Emmett

S.M.A.R.T. Goals make dreams come true.

This one step – choosing a goal and sticking to it – changes everything. Scott Reed

MY LIFE MAP

Unlike a road map, a **Life Map** may have many parts. If you are focusing on a few different goals, you will then need to copy this page and do the activity a number of times.

My Long-Term Goal is:

(My destination based upon my dreams)

My Intermediate Goals are:

(Based upon my activity storms)

My Short-Term Goals are:

My Immediate Goals are:

Commitment is the key to unlocking the door to your dreams! You must commit to your goals. Tracy Lyn Moland

Goals of Moms

Save enough money to purchase a new vehicle. *Kathy*

To clean out the storage room. *Barbara*

To get a part time job. *Kathy*

To get back into shape. *Mom*

Success with my new home-based business. *Val*

To get laundry done! *Stephanie*

My goal right now is to find a happy place for me. *Pam*

To pay off our debt. *Mom*

To make it through the day without yelling at my children. *Mom*

To find a job closer to home so that I'm spending less time commuting and more time with my family. *Mom*

To lose weight. *Mom*

To be financially secure. *Madeline*

To find a comfort level in my life that balances every part of the three most important things in my life. *Tammy*

S.M.A.R.T Goals

Find time for myself. I am going to have an outing or take a class one night/day per week. I will organize this within one month. *Cathleen*

To create enough inventory for an upcoming juried artist's studio tour in the fall. *Jan*

To do two triathlons in one year. *Michelle*

Now that we have created our **Life Map** based upon our dreams and goals, we need to look at our life as it is today and determine how these new commitments will fit into our lifestyle. In the next chapter, we will look at the many different roles we assume as Mothers and make room for our new priorities.

Desire is the key to motivation, but it's an unrelenting pursuit of your goal — a commitment to excellence - that will enable you to attain the success you seek. Mario Andretti

---

How Many Pairs of Shoes Can You Wear at Once?

Balancing Life's Multiple Roles

HOW MANY DIFFERENT PAIRS OF SHOES ARE YOU WEARING?

How many roles do you assume in life? I like to use shoes as an analogy of our roles plus this gives me an excuse to buy more pairs—research for the book, of course!

I wear a lot of shoes in my life. Some are chosen and some are given to me! Are you ready for the list? Here are my shoes!

> Mom, wife, daughter, sister, aunt, daughter-in-law, friend, cousin, acquaintance, associate, contact, triathlete, swimmer, runner, biker, instructor, director, facilitator, speaker, author, entrepreneur, consultant, manager, cook, cleaner, cab driver, researcher, volunteer, teacher, tutor, designer, maid, host, psychologist, ...

Life is about balance! If you can find a balance between the many roles you assume in your life, you will find a balance in your well-being – and the **Life Map** you have now created will be much more enjoyable!

Be aware of wonder. Live a balanced life – learn some and think some and draw and paint and sing and dance and play and work everyday some. Robert Fulghum

What does Balance mean?

In the Webster's Dictionary, some of the different meanings of balance include, "5a: stability produced by even distribution of weight on each side of the vertical axis; 9: mental and emotional steadiness."

In our lives, balance is about finding stability and steadiness in the roles we play in life. There is a balance between the shoes we wear as a mother and an employee. There is a balance between finding time for me, time as a couple, time as a family and time for everything else. Balance does not mean doing only the fun things. Imagine our diet for a minute. We each have our favourite food or type of food. I love to eat out and always wish I could eat out more. Awhile back, I ate out for seven meals in a row with the seventh being lunch on my birthday. Since it was my birthday, my family wanted to take me out for supper that night, but I just couldn't do it! I could NOT eat another meal out. I had had enough (for that week at least).

While all of our roles come with many rewarding tasks, they also come with necessary tasks. I love the way I feel when I am fit, but I don't always love to work out. Sometimes the weights just feel too heavy or the run feels too long. However, if I want to receive the benefits of being fit, I have to do what is necessary.

The Role of Mom

Rewarding	Necessary
Cuddles, hugs, quiet time, game time, activities, trips, "I love you, Mommy", firsts, seconds, achievements, milestones, one on one outings, talking, sharing, growing, eating together… The list goes on!	Cleaning, cooking, driving, whining, scolding, discipline, mediation, homework helper, conflict resolution, listening, volunteering, fundraising, accounting, laundry, employee, party planner… The list goes on!

How Do We Find Balance?

What do we need to do to find balance? Especially when we feel like we have too many pairs of shoes (is that possible?), and many of those are uncomfortable to wear at best. We are off to a head start because at this point of our Mom

Management journey, we have taken the first few steps. We have created a *Life Map*.

This *Life Map* has helped us to determine our priorities. We have started to understand what is most important to our families, our lives, and ourselves.

We now need to take a look at our life as it is today. Until we can determine where we are right now in life, we cannot move forward and make changes. We need to decide if we are balanced and if not, determine what we need to do to find balance between our roles. Once we know this, we can start to add, remove or adjust roles so that we can bring our dreams and priorities into our daily life.

You don't set the course for where you are going until you know where you are. Unknown.

WHO WE ARE VS WHAT WE DO

Who we ARE is often found in the titles and descriptions of our roles. These generally do not change. For example, Mom, wife or sister.	What we Do is often based upon who we are. There are certain tasks associated with roles in life. For example, teach, clean, discipline.

Activity

1. LIST all the different shoes you wear in life (all the roles you assume).

2. DIVIDE them into *Who You Are* and *What You Do*. Some things aren't really clear so if you are not sure, put them in the middle.

<u>Who I AM</u>   <u>What I DO</u>

Now:

- **Cirde** the **5** things you **DO/ARE** the most
- <u>Underline</u> the **5** things you **DO/ARE** the least
- Put a **Star** beside your **5** favorite roles
- Put a ~~line through~~ your **5** least favorite roles

49

3. ASK YOURSELF some key questions:

Are the things I do most often my favorites?

Are the things I do most often my least favorite?

How often am I doing my favorites?

Are my favorite things "who I am"?

Are my least favorite things "what I do"?

Do my favorites match with my dreams and goals? If not, why?

Do I need to add some new roles to my life in order to reach my dreams? What are they?

Take a few minutes right now and ADD them to your list.

Are you confusing priorities with importance?

Often, when we go through our lists of roles we find we are doing a number of important things. When we are not aware of our priorities, we fill our lives with things that are important but we need to ask ourselves if they are really important to us.

Take volunteering for example. There are many wonderful opportunities for us to volunteer. We can't say 'Yes' to them all. We need to choose what is right for us. I volunteer for the YMCA, as well as sit on a board of directors. Both allow me to commit to organizations I believe in while growing and learning. They both fall in line with my priorities of fitness. I also help out at my children's school, which is an important part of my family role.

When asked to do more volunteering, I have to make a decision. Unless I am willing to let go of something else, I need to and do say 'No'.

So even if some of your roles seem extremely important, unless they are in line with your priorities and are important to you, you should not be doing them.

There are so many important things to do and be in the world; we need to choose what is important to us and then commit to it. Tracy Lyn Moland

---

FOCUS ROLES

Take a few minutes and look back at your *Life Map* – your dreams and goals. Based upon your *Life Map*, determine the five roles you need to focus on. It is okay to group some of the activities together as I have below. However, if you make the roles so broad that they each are overwhelming, it won't make a difference. These roles need to be your top priorities and you need to have them written down. You need to take them with you and refer to them daily. Then when you are asked to take on a new role you can determine if it fits with your focus. If it does, find a non-priority item to delete and add it. If not, you have a reason to say '*No*'.

Tracy Lyn's Five Focus Roles are:

1. Myself – this includes taking care of me and maintaining my fitness level.

2. Mother

3. Wife

4. Work – my speaking & writing

5. Relationships – with family and friends

I enjoy my job and it gives me an identity beyond that of being a wife and a mother. A surveyed Mom

Based upon my dreams and goals, the five roles I need to focus upon in life are:

1. Myself - I have chosen this one for you. This book is about taking care of the Me in Mommeee so it should be one of your priorities.

2.

3.

4.

5.

MAKING CHANGES TO YOUR LIST

Now that you have determined the five main roles you want to focus on, you need to start removing roles from your list. There are things you can change and things you cannot change. As I noted above, the job description for the roles we *are* is full of things we *do*. Moms' favorite roles usually include things they are and their least favorites things they do. Part of being a Mom involves driving your children around or helping them with homework, so as you decide to remove items from your list think about how they relate to your focus roles.

Often, just by understanding the connection between something that you DO and one of your focus roles, your perspective will change. Rather than being frustrated at some of the duties of being a Mom, you will feel grateful that you have the opportunity to be there for your family.

Methods of Removing Roles

After having determined your *focus* roles, you need to decide what to do about the other roles. This is the time to determine which roles you want to remove from your list. Removing roles includes delegation and learning to say '*No*'.

There are three ways to get something done: do it yourself, hire someone, or forbid your kids to do it. Monta Crane

Delegation

You can't remove the role of Mom or sister from your list, but do you have to perform all the duties associated with these roles? You can hire someone to clean your house, you can car pool, or you can delegate jobs to your family or partner. Many Moms have goals of raising happy and responsible children. As you delegate, you provide these opportunities for your family to learn.

1. DECIDE WHAT YOU CAN DELEGATE: family chores, job duties, and volunteer duties. Sometimes you need to delegate jobs you enjoy. Look at your priorities. Is there a better use of your time? Is it time for your children or your assistant to learn this new skill? If you only delegate the unpleasant jobs, you cannot learn and improve your own skills nor can your helpers.

2. PICK THE RIGHT PERSON FOR THE JOB – your three-year-old cannot make supper but it is a learning opportunity for a 12-year-old.

Potato Soup! I remember the first time Mom had me cook dinner… the entire dinner. I decided to prepare mashed potatoes. I added in a bit of milk and then a bit more. It just wasn't enough so in went two entire cups… guess what, we didn't have mashed potatoes that night. This was the first of many mistakes, as cooking one meal a week became a regular chore for me. Mom got some help and I learned kitchen skills.

3. TRY TO DELEGATE THE ENTIRE JOB. If your son is in charge of garbage day, he collects the garbage and recyclables, puts them out and brings in the empty

cans at the end. Let whomever you delegate to take on the entire project.

4. ACCEPT ONLY FINISHED WORK but be there as a coach. You can answer questions about how to cook chili or what is the best rag to use for dusting, but don't be critical of your children, partner, assistant or anyone if they have done the best job they can. If you re-do the job after, then what is the point of delegating? Standards may be different and you need to accept theirs. If you have specific requirements, let them know ahead of time or next time. Learn to have patience when delegating.

5. GIVE CREDIT! Make sure to give credit and praise after the job is complete, especially to our partners and children, as we want to make sure they do it again!

6. INCLUDE SOME DELEGATING IN ALL YOUR ROLES. Make sure to delegate at home, work or in volunteer positions. People need to learn, and you need to learn to delegate!

You must be willing to let go of your fear of losing control and learn to delegate tasks and projects so that you can have more time for yourself. Stephanie Culp

---

Ways Moms are already delegating:

I am very fortunate that my husband does most of the household chores. *Lisa*

Hire a babysitter. *Trish*

Hire someone to do it for you. *Wendy*

You'd be surprised that asking for help actually works! *Kathy*

One Mother sums it up perfectly, "Delegate – everyone should help out, no matter how young. As the kids get older, they can help more!"

Learn to Say No

You can do it... and now you understand the reasons why you *should* do it. If you respect yourself, then you respect your dreams and goals. You have created a **Life Map** and you know the five main roles you need to focus upon to live your life of balance. Keep these with you at all times, put your collage up by your phone, and use these items as a constant reminder that you can say 'No' to the constant requests you receive.

Ways to Say No

1. USE YOUR PLANNER. You will have your goals and activities scheduled in and can say, "I am booked already". This includes personal time. It is just as important to respect yourself by including time for a massage or a lunch date with a friend, as it is to include time for a work meeting or doctor's appointment.

2. REFER TO YOUR LIST OF FIVE FOCUS ROLES. If the request doesn't fit in with your focus you have to say '*No*'. The volunteer example above works here.

3. SAY *NO* TO THE REQUEST, NOT THE PERSON. It is a great cause but I can't help with silent auction right now.

4. POSTPONE YOUR REPLY. It may be easier to say, 'I will think about it', and then say 'No' later. Allow your decisions to be pro-active (in your control) rather than re-active (in someone else's control). This gives you a chance to look at your **Life Map** and see if this opportunity fits. Sometimes you need to say '*No*' to great opportunities as well. I was invited to a free ski day as a volunteer appreciation gift. As much as I love to ski, I had to say '*No*' to the opportunity because I had a presentation the next day. I felt that a day of skiing

would not leave me prepared for one of my main priorities – my speaking career.

5. FIND ANOTHER SOLUTION. I can't take the time to do that right now but I could make a donation of money or a product.

6. REMIND YOURSELF. If you are going to add a new role, then you need to remove an old role.

Choosing to say 'No' is often the best strategy to keep your life well balanced and in control. Les Hewit, Jack Canfield, and Mark Victor Hansen

---

MULTI-TASKING

As women, we were born with the amazing skill of multi-tasking. We can wear two or three different pairs of shoes at once. When we became Mothers, we perfected this skill. Who else but a Mom can talk on the phone, make supper, help her children with homework, and answer the doorbell at the same time! Moms all over the world provided ideas for this book on how to simplify their lives by multi-tasking.

There are times when we need to learn *not* to multi-task. Some activities require full concentration. I once looked over at a car driving beside me; the man was reading a book. I drove away from him quickly. Often, if it is a safety issue we will concentrate, but there are many more occasions that require our full concentration.

Multi-Tasking Moms

I watch hockey and do up my Avon orders.

I take a bath and read my favourite magazine.

I listen to cassette tapes while crafting or driving.

I fold laundry while watching TV.

I listen to books on tape while commuting.

I read while waiting for my kids to finish activities.

Avoid Multi-Tasking During:

1. ACTIVITIES THAT REQUIRE YOU TO THINK - I can talk to my Mom on the phone and wash dishes while giving her my full attention, but I cannot talk on the phone and send an email at the same time. Both require my full attention. If you realize you have no idea what someone said on the phone, or what you just read, then you need to focus on these activities. This is an important skill to teach your children, especially during homework time!

2. IMPORTANT ACTIVITIES - Be aware of multi-tasking during the following types of activities: meetings, appointments, important phone calls, health/fitness issues, driving, business/work activities,

safety issues, homework, research and most importantly, diaper changing!

3. PERSONAL TIME, FAMILY TIME AND COUPLE TIME - If you do not solely concentrate on these, they will not happen. If I am working on my laptop during our family movie night, then it isn't really family time. If you take the kids out for dinner during a couple night, it isn't really couple time anymore. If you take the kids in the bubble bath with you, you won't recharge.

As Moms we have a number of different shoes we need to wear, and still others we want to wear. At times we may have too many, and other times we may feel the need to wear different shoes on each foot! If we have taken the time to determine our priorities and our focus roles, it will make our lives run smoother and our **Life Map** much more realistic. Our goal is to find a balance between our roles and not try to do it all. If you still find yourself struggling for balance, see if the tips in the next chapter are helpful to you.

Ways Moms Found to Focus on
Some of Their Roles!

Partner Time

We have a date night once a month. We book the babysitter weeks in advance. *Hyla*

We go for breakfast every Friday morning. *Helene*

I like to put everything else aside after the kids have gone to bed and that is my time to do something for me or with my husband. *Cathy*

My theory is that our family is here because of the relationship my husband and I have. If we want our family to be strong and emotionally healthy, our relationship must (at times) come first. We do this by traveling alone at least twice a year. *Lori*

Family Time

I turn ordinary events into special occasions. *Deb*

During family dinners, we light candles for each person and everyone talks about the best thing they did that day. *Christine*

We designate a time and day as family day/time. NO excuses or exceptions! *Trish*

Ok, So Now What?

Eliminating Time Wasters

A bend in the road is not the end of the road -- unless you fail to make the turn. Unknown

---

Ok, so now what? Sure I know what my dreams are. I have a **Life Map** filled with goals to help me achieve my dreams. I know the roles in life I need to focus upon and I even know how to say *No* and delegate. But - and this is a big BUT - I have no time. As a Mom Manager I am so busy I don't even know where to start and where to fit these activities into my life!

Do you feel this way? Hopefully not but I bet there are times when you think I must be crazy even suggesting these ideas. How can she be a real Mom Manager? I must admit I experience trying times, but in general I live the life I describe in this book. Because I have created my **Life Map** and know my priorities, I can handle the *off* times. I know where they are leading me.

If you really feel you don't have time to implement some of the activities in this book, keep on reading this chapter. See if you can find at least one way to regain some control over your time so you can fit in one or two activities that will lead to your dreams.

TIME WASTERS

Do you know how much time we waste? There are so many things we do *just because*, and not for any particular reason at all. The average person watches hours and hours of TV per week. We worry so much about what we should do next that we don't end up doing anything at all. This chapter is filled with the ways we waste time and methods we can implement to eliminate them.

Time wasted is existence; time used is life. Edward Young

Perfectionism... *a disposition to regard anything short of perfection as unacceptable.* Webster's Dictionary

How much time is wasted when we are trying to achieve perfection? And how often is it actually achieved? I can think of very few things that are 100% perfect. Think of cooking – many people don't measure their ingredients to perfection but still turn out excellent foods.

Striving for excellence motivates you; striving for perfection is demoralizing. Harriet Braiker

We often spend so much time trying to be perfect we let life pass us by. As a mother of five suggests, "Your kids are only little for a short time. Enjoy them while they are there." Striving to be perfect can be so damaging to our lives that we can miss out on what is really important.

Recently at the wedding of a friend of the family, I listened as our Mothers reminisced about a comment made many years ago, "What do you think the kids will remember more - our nights of playing games or a clean house?" They were right, I have no idea how clean my house was but we sure had fun every Friday night watching *The Dukes of Hazard* and playing games.

Aim For Completion Or Excellence

Depending on the situation, rather than perfection, we need to aim for completion or excellence. Some jobs simply need to be completed and others need to be done well – within our own measure of excellence, but not perfect.

When house cleaning, will it really matter if there is a streak on our mirror, or is it more important that the house feels clean? Books have an average of seven mistakes in them. If my aim was to present the *perfect* book, I would still be revising this book.

If we are guilty of always aiming for perfection, before starting tasks, we need to set limits. Our limits can either be determined by time, by a set quantity or a level of success. For example, I will clean for one hour or I will only re-do this job two times.

The person who never makes a mistake probably isn't doing anything. Rita Emmett

---

Activity

In what areas do I feel the need to be perfect?

Order in the house & cleanliness but end up overwhelmed

How can I re-focus my attention on completion rather than perfection?

Set a timer, break up tasks into parts or days to do, make a check list. Simplify to make it easier & faster, purge what I own. Make a daily schedule

DETAILS, DETAILS, DETAILS

How many colors of lipstick, types of cereal or magazines are there? How many houses are there to buy? We are lucky to live in a time when we have so many choices. We also waste a great deal of time making decisions. For example, I have counted 1082 different colors of lipstick at a local pharmacy. There is moisturizing, shiny, glossy, matte, shimmers, and countless other types to choose from. We could spend hours picking the *right* color… is it worth our time?

Our life is frittered away by details...Simplify, simplify.
Henry David Thoreau

Most decisions we have to make in life are not life or death decisions. If we buy a lipstick that doesn't look good, we can throw it away. If an outfit doesn't fit, we can return it. If a recipe doesn't work, we won't try it again.

When we are faced with decisions, we need to think about the outcome. If the outcome is not a big deal, doesn't cause hurt feelings or injury, and does not involve a great deal of money, then we should make a quick decision.

Sandi Richard, also known as Canada's Meal Planning Expert, has taken the details out of meals. In her "Cooking for the Rushed" series of cookbooks, she provides a meal planning system that is as much about stress reduction as it is about creating healthy, delicious, and quick suppers. She has simplified both grocery shopping and healthy eating for thousands of people. See www.CookingfortheRushed.com for more information.

Big Decisions

There are decisions that are worth taking time to make. These decisions usually save time and money in the end. When making big purchases like cars or houses, you need to spend some time making sure you get what is best for you. Always use a *'what if'* scenario to help you with decisions. Think about what would happen if you made a hasty decision and use that as your guide to how much time you should spend. **BUT** remember, don't wait for the perfect decision.

Nothing will ever be attempted if all possible objections must first be overcome. Samuel Johnson

Activity

What is my decision-making style?

Does this match with the style of my partner or family?

Which decisions do I spend too much time worrying about?

How can I change how I make my decisions?

My husband and I are completely different at making decisions. I like to make a quick decision and get it over with. Pat likes to think about things. He likes to make sure it is the right item, the right price, the right color, the right style, etc. A few years ago we were looking at getting a bigger TV. We went into all the electronic shops – many times. We talked price, we talked product and we finally picked out the TV we wanted. For some reason though, we just kept going back to look at it and never bought it. Finally, I couldn't stand it anymore so I went out and bought the TV for Pat for Father's Day

While our differing decision-making attitudes can clash, they have been beneficial. If it weren't for Pat we would end up with a lot of things we don't need or really want. If it weren't for me we would still be thinking about that TV!

We have also learned from each other - I will take some time to think about decisions and he makes the effort to be more spontaneous.

PROCRASTINATION

Okay, I am going to write this later! Procrastination is one of the biggest time wasters of all. Rita Emmett has written an entire book on this topic. If it is one of your *bad habits*, I highly recommend reading, *The Procrastinator's Handbook,* (Random House, 2000).

There are two things to consider in eliminating procrastination:

1. WHY we do it?
2. What we NEED TO DO to PREVENT it.

Often when we figure out WHY we do something, the procrastination problem is resolved. In seminars, I have asked groups of people why they procrastinate. The list is usually very similar and includes the following:

Why Do People Procrastinate?

FEAR of failure	WE are lazy
FEAR of success	WE don't care
LACK of knowledge	The TASK is unpleasant
NOT sure *how* to do the task	The TASK is dull
NOT sure of *what* to do	The TASK is overwhelming
LACK of focus	The TASK lacks urgency

Hard work is often the easy work you did not do at the proper time. Bernard Meltzer

Once we have determined the why, we may know how to solve the problem. We can just get going and get the job done. Or we can decide that we don't really need to do it and remove it from our To Do list.

If, after we have determined WHY, we still can't get going the following ideas should help:

Methods to Prevent Procrastination

1. PLAN AND PRIORITIZE your To-do lists, schedules, dreams, and goals. Organize your life. Follow the steps in chapters eight, nine and ten.

2. BREAK A LARGE JOB INTO SMALLER JOBS and do them step-by-step. Take cleaning your house as an example. For most of us, this is a huge, time-consuming task that we would rather avoid. To simplify the job a number of Moms surveyed divided their chores into daily duties – bathrooms on Sunday, dust on Monday, and vacuum on Tuesday.

3. SET A TIME LIMIT. Work on a project for one hour and then stop. Ignore the phone and email and work for the set amount of time. This works even better if you schedule these chunks of time into your schedule.

4. GIVE YOURSELF PERMISSION TO QUIT. If there is a job you know you must do but just don't feel like it, start, and give yourself permission to quit in 15 minutes. Usually at the end of the 15 minutes you will be into it and will continue on. If not, you have made some progress, and next time you work on it you are that much farther ahead. This also works really well with exercise.

5. TAKE ADVANTAGE OF POCKETS OF TIME to make a dent in a project. If you have 10 minutes between appointments, why not make two of the eight calls you need to make. Write Christmas cards during naptime or a hockey practice. Wash dishes while you are on the phone. I learned a great habit from my Mom - whenever she had to wait, she would clean out her purse. Carry books or articles from magazines with you so you can get them read while you have to wait.

6. REWARD YOURSELF. Plan a suitable reward for completion of a job or task. Suitable is the key word here - a trip to Mexico because you cleaned the

bathroom is probably not a good choice but a bubble bath would be a great idea!

7. CREATE DEADLINES. Inviting company over is a surefire way to get the house tidied. Make an appointment with a client to review some work. Invite your Mother-In-Law over. Sign up for a 5km run. Book a holiday.

8. CREATE SYSTEMS. Are there things you do over and over again? Do you find yourself procrastinating because you have done something so often it seems easy or it is boring? Create re-usable systems. Photocopy and re-use your grocery lists, chore charts, Christmas card list, etc.

Putting off an easy thing makes it hard, and putting off a hard one makes it impossible. George H Lonmer

---

Activity

What things do I usually procrastinate about?

Why am I procrastinating?

Which of the above methods would help me stop procrastinating?

CLUTTER AND DISORGANIZATION

"Mom, you are always looking for your keys!" My daughter's comment finally persuaded me that it was time to get a key rack. Almost every time we went out, I had the panic and the stress of a key hunt. Usually I found them, although there was that three-month period when my then two-year-old put them in a cup in the back of a rarely used cupboard. I now have a funky looking key rack at the door with keys hanging on it. What a difference! I almost always know where my keys are now.

How much time is wasted looking for things? I have spent weeks of my life looking for things. It is so frustrating and we feel so stressed until we finally find them.

How often have you been stressed out when trying to decide where to put the forks? Or how about your socks?

Before we worry about what we can't find, we need to think about what we can find. We all have a place to put our socks and our cutlery so why not find a place for everything? We will go into detail on this in chapter ten.

Put things in their proper place and if you can't find it in the first 30 seconds, it's not in the correct place. Harwant Johnson

Activity

What can you always find?

What are you always looking for?

Where is a logical place to keep these things?

NO LIFE MAP

If you don't know where you are going, every road will get you nowhere. Henry Kissinger

Chapters two through five have helped you to create your **Life Map**. You know what is important and what you should you be doing. You know that if something doesn't fit in with your five most important roles that you shouldn't do it.

If you still find that you don't have enough time or aren't focusing on your priorities, you need to go back through the exercises in those chapters. Things may have changed or you may have not chosen true priorities. Perhaps you have chosen too many dreams or goals to focus on? Choose which ones you want to do now and which ones you will do later. Be sure to commit to these goals and get started. Don't wait for the *right* time, as there is no *right* time.

Watch out for these time wasters that will get you when you haven't set your priorities:

TV	Negative People
Telephone	Junk Mail
Email	Clutter
Internet	Overanalysing
Gossip	Video Games
Worry	Interruptions

Time you enjoyed wasting is not wasted time.
T.S. Elliot

Do keep this quote in mind. Be aware of the difference between relaxing or having fun and literally wasting time. Watching a favorite TV show is fine on occasion – it is when you flip for hours, don't enjoy it and then complain you have no time, that you are truly wasting time and need to avoid it.

Activity

1. Review the **Life Map** that you created in Chapter four and see if you need to re-do the activities or if you just need to implement them.

TOO MUCH OF A GOOD THING

Yes, you can have too much of a good thing. Imagine just eating chocolate or potato chips for the rest of your life. At first you may enjoy it but before long you would be sick of chocolate (at least I assume so!). I used to diet and I must admit chocolate bars tasted so much better then. Now we have left over chocolate bars in the freezer from the past two Halloweens and I have no desire to eat them!

Doing too much of a good thing can also be a monumental time waster. While attending university, my roommate and I always had the cleanest bathrooms during finals. Following are some examples of some of the things Moms do too much of:

TOO MUCH VOLUNTEERING. There are many good causes and reasons to volunteer, but you can't do them all. You need to choose.

TOO MUCH TIME HELPING OTHERS. I know people who will do everything they can to help others and never take care of themselves. Even if it isn't too much there is a time that Moms need to let go and let their children do things for themselves. I recently heard coach Martha Beck author of *Finding Your Own North Star,* Three Rivers Press, suggesting that our role as parents is to teach our children to do things and then let them do it.

TOO MANY ACTIVITIES. Trying to do it all at once will lead to burnout. Just like our children, we can't participate in everything.

TOO MANY GOALS, DREAMS OR PRIORITIES. Often when we try to do everything we dream of, we find ourselves not doing any of them. Or we end up burning ourselves out; getting sick or so frustrated we figure goal setting just doesn't work. I had to let my triathlon goals go the year I wrote this book. I just could not commit to producing a book and training for triathlons.

Don't let your life be like a treadmill – sure it is good for you but you never actually go anywhere!

Lucy Maud Montgomery puts a different perspective on this idea of too much in her book, Anne of Green Gables: *"After all," Anne said to Marilla once, "I believe the nicest and sweetest days are not those on which anything very splendid or wonderful or exciting happens but those that bring simple little pleasures, following one another softly, like pearls slipping off a string."*

Make sure you also make room for down time. We all (family included) need to take time to relax, re-coupe, re-cover, and re-charge.

Activity

What are you doing too much of?

What can you let go of to find more balance in your life?

Though usually I am an amazing sleeper, the other night sleep decided that it wasn't going to visit me. Usually I find that so frustrating but this night was different. I was calm, relaxed and I was inspired. An entire keynote address came to me. Answers to some questions I had been pondering formalized themselves so clearly. I got up and wrote some of the information down. The rest, I went over and over in my mind, clarifying the details and in the morning wrote them down. Rather than being mad about a night of no sleep, I am so thankful that I was given the chance to be inspired.

As I tell this story to other women, I have heard many similar stories. Many amazing ideas and creations have come on a sleepless night or in the bathtub!

Sometimes you must slow down to go faster. Ann McGee Cooper

PEOPLE

This is a bit of an awkward section to write. Have you taken time to look at whom you spend your time with? We are very affected by the people around us. Think of the people you know – friends, family, acquaintances, co-workers, or people you run into regularly and try the following exercise:

1. Think of the people you really ENJOY spending time with — even if it is a brief hello at the cash register at the grocery store.

2. Now think of the people that you dread seeing, avoid being around or just simply don't care for.

3. What is it that you like about the people in question one? How do they make you feel? How do you feel after they leave?

4. What is it that you don't like about the people in question two? How do they make you feel? How do you feel after they leave?

The only way to have a friend is to be one. Ralph Waldo Emerson

---

Mentors

It is documented time-and-time again that you are like the people you spend the most time with. In business, people are encouraged to find mentors to learn from. A definition of mentor is: A wise and trusted counsellor or teacher. I have had many mentors in life including many teachers. In writing this book I had the help of many wonderful mentors, including: Patricia Cobe, Ellen H. Parlapiano, Sandi Richard, Jenny Hoops and Tim Breithaupt. Their help has been invaluable and has made a difference to my life and the quality of this book.

It is also important to be a mentor. As I have worked with women entrepreneurs my own skills have increased dramatically. I have learned a lot about myself through teaching and mentoring others. Both sides of the relationships are very satisfying.

See if you can find a way to bring mentoring into your life. It could be as simple as an exercise buddy or being there to support a friend. You could work with your own children or with your partner. If there is someone you would like to be like, spend some time with him or her. For more ideas on mentoring, read *The Power of Focus* by Les Hewitt, Jack Canfield and Mark Victor Hansen, Heath Communications, Inc.

TAKE A LOOK AROUND

Be aware of the relationships that surround you in your day-to-day life. If you find yourself surrounded by negative people, then you are bound to feel the same. Try to spend most of your time with positive people.

Now I do realize that you don't have total control over all of the people in your life. You may have relatives, friends, co-workers, or neighbors that are at times negative or hard to be around. You may find that if you are doing things differently than your parents you may not receive full support from them. You may not even have full support from your partner. Often, these are still people you want in your life, so by being aware of your feelings, you can plan and prepare accordingly. If family gatherings leave you feeling frustrated and overwhelmed, maybe a coffee with a girlfriend the next day would be a great way to bring the positive back. Or why not go for a run before you get there? Why not change the activity you do with the person - if you have a friend or relative that leaves you feeling down, why not go to a movie together instead of dinner?

There is also a time when some relationships need to be terminated. If someone always brings you down or selfishly dismisses your dreams or goals it may be time to move on and make new friends.

Save your precious time for the people that mean the most to you. People that support you, make you feel good, make you laugh, share your joy and sorrow, and are kindred spirits.

Until we take how we see ourselves (and how we see others) into account, we will be unable to understand how others see and feel about themselves and their world. Unaware, we will project our intentions on their behavior and call ourselves objective. Stephen Covey

---

> *Assessment* – Are you the one who is negative or competitive? Are you the one who is hard to be with? Are you the one who does all the talking and never listens? Are you the one who is so self-absorbed?

Kindred spirits are not so scarce as I used to think. It's splendid to find out there are so many of them in the world.
Elizabeth Von Arnim

Find your kindred spirits! Be a kindred spirit.

HIDDEN TIME

One of the greatest time wasters is unaccounted for time. We have a pretty good idea of how long things take us to do but we don't always think about the time that surrounds the activity. When I go for a workout, my goal is to exercise for one hour. This is how much time it actually takes.

One-Hour Workout
20 minutes travel time to the gym
20 minutes to drop the kids into childcare and get changed
60 minutes to exercise
30 minutes to shower, change and pick up the kids
20 minutes travel time home
Total = 2 hours 30 minutes

Most of us would only book one hour in our planner for this workout yet it actually takes two and a half hours. Think about all the things that require extra time that must be calculated into them. Next time you plan an activity, think about these other time factors:

Travel time – Don't forget to include time to park the car, get the kids out and ready, walk to the door, enter the building, and get to your destination. We often only think about the actual commuting time and forget that we need to allow another 5-10 minutes to get from the parking lot or bus stop to our actual destination.

Preparation time - When I do a presentation, I need to get there early to make sure that my equipment is ready, to get a feel for the room, and to have time to relax and feel ready.

Clean up time – In my daughter's kindergarten class the teacher always stopped all activities 30 minutes before the bell rang. This ensured there was adequate clean up time.

Grooming time – If you have teenage girls, you already know about this! If you have to leave at 10 o'clock, you need to start to get the kids and yourself ready long before that.

Break time – No matter what we are doing, we need to make sure to factor in some break time. I remember a professor in university saying that your mind can only work for

45 minutes before it needs a change of pace. We each have our own limit but no matter what we are doing, at some point we need to take a break.

Unexpected time – I always give myself extra time to get to places. I like to allow for a few 'what ifs' – last minute phone call, traffic tie up, bad weather, kids forgetting something (okay it is usually me forgetting something!), bathroom breaks, etc.

> I have always liked a good deal. I love looking through flyers on Sundays and seeing what is available but I have learned to be as picky about my time as I am about my money. If I take into account all the travel time, it just doesn't make sense to go to three different grocery stores to save a few dollars. It makes more sense for me to pick the one with the overall best deals and go there.

Activity

What are the time components I am forgetting when I plan and schedule activities?

For the next few weeks try keeping track of how long things actually take. Then use this information to help you better track your time.

<u>Activity</u>

Questions you should ask yourself to prevent wasting time:

Does this need to be perfect or just completed?

Am I wasting time making decisions? Can I eliminate some of the details?

When I am procrastinating about a task, can I figure out *why* I am doing it? What method would work on this task?

Does everything have a place to go? Am I wasting time looking for the same thing over and over? Am I frustrated by the mess and the clutter?

Am I doing too much of a good thing? Is there one thing taking over my life? Do I need down time?

Who am I spending my time with? How do they make me feel? Do I have a mentor? Am I a mentor? Who are my kindred spirits?

Am I taking into account how long things actually take? Am I remembering to include the time that surrounds all activities?

Now that we have figured out some ways to eliminate time wasters, we need to use that time for something very important – us! In the next chapter, we will determine ways to include **Me Time** into our daily schedules.

Me Time

Time Alone

Mom Manager, through this journey, have you found the time to be alone? Have you been doing more than just reading this book? Have you been reading this book in the bathtub? Have you been taking a few minutes here and there to fill in your dream list? Have you made sure to include yourself in your list of multiple roles? Are you taking Time for You? This chapter is your reminder to remember to put on your oxygen mask first.

ME TIME

The dream of every Mom is to have some time alone. Last summer, my husband took the kids away for a weekend and I was in heaven. It was wonderful to be alone in my own house and to do what I wanted. I made a commitment to myself not to clean a thing – but I sure got a lot of organizing and major projects finished. I also watched a few movies and slept in! By the end of the weekend I was completely recharged and ready for some noise and hugs.

Mom Management

Moms get lost in the shuffle of life at times and are often afraid to admit we need help. We fear we will look inadequate if we use outside services like childcare, an errand service or a house cleaner. We feel guilty if we dare to take even a moment for ourselves. We think everyone else has it together except us. We all strive to be *Super Mom* yet we are more successful when we are *Balanced Mom*.

If women were convinced that a day off or an hour of solitude was a reasonable ambition, they would find a way of attaining it. As it is, they feel so unjustified in their demand that they rarely make the attempt. Anne Morrow Lindbergh

---

Many days it seems impossible to get some time alone to recharge and balance, and those are the days when it is absolutely necessary. And I know exactly what you are thinking, "How can I possibly take some time for me? The kids are too young, too old too busy, too demanding, too…" My mom used to tell me I needed to take an hour a day for me. I just laughed. I couldn't even begin to figure out exactly which hour I would use - the one at 4:00 am or the one at midnight! But what about sleep? Oh well, maybe tomorrow or maybe when the kids are in university.

We often say, "I can't find time for myself." Yet there are many occasions in which we find the time we need for other things. We, as mothers, often don't feel we deserve this time unless we have a *reason*. Yet, if we or one of our children were very sick, we would find the time to go to the doctor. We find the time to get our haircut, to attend school interviews, to mow the lawn, to wash the dishes, to plan birthdays, to take the car to the garage, etc.

Next time you have to find time for something, pay attention to how you did it. Now apply this skill to taking care of you before you really do get sick and are forced to care for yourself.

My Mom was right and by doing the exercises I suggest in this book, I have figured out ways to find this time alone. I consider my writing and presenting as my **Me Time** because I am doing work that I love.

Trust is one of the keys to finding **Me Time**. We have to have full confidence that our children are being cared for. Our partners have their own way of doing things and that is okay. So what if they forget the diaper bag (which my husband has) or take the kids for junk food after band practice? If we complain about what our partners or parents do while we are out, they won't help us again. We need to make sure to choose childcare we trust and then we need to go out and enjoy our time.

Types of Me Time

There is definitely a difference in the methods Moms with young children use to find more time than Moms with teens use. There are days it is almost impossible to find even one minute with little babies around. We do need to be creative — nap time, trade childcare with a neighbor, or watch our favorite TV show on tape while breast-feeding. As our children grow and don't need to be held or cared for all the time, there are more opportunities available for Moms to find some **Me Time**. But we still need to be creative. It doesn't come naturally. As one mother explains, "I am finding time for myself more and more, BUT I'm finding that I have to snatch those pockets of time as they come. Now the kids are especially busy, more so then when they were little. During the day I find time between chores, errands and picking up kids at school or attending their events."

Moms with younger children finding Me Time

My **Me Time** is when I go to the gym where there is childcare. *Natalie*

I have my partner take care of our baby when he gets home from work. *Mom*

I take **Me Time** when my children are napping. *Mom*

Lock the bathroom door when taking a shower and make sure you have the key! *Gwen*

Moms with teens finding Me Time

Talk to your teens about respecting your quiet time in the evening. *Patrice*

Commit to a bible study group. *Mom*

I book my hairdressing and exercise session in my day timer just like any other appointment, including my dates (I'm a single Mom). *Tara*

Bath time is sacred. *Mom*

I use my morning before anyone gets up to meditate and get centered. *Mom*

When we start to take **Me Time**, we often feel we need to justify this time. However, as we continue to do it, we begin to see how valuable it is. We see the difference it makes to our families and our families see the difference it makes in us.

Love yourself first and everything else falls in line. Lucille Ball

---

Taking some time for yourself is not being selfish. You cannot be happy and successful if you are tired, sick and stressed out. You need *Me Time*.

Webster's dictionary defines selfishness as being "Concerned excessively or exclusively with oneself: seeing or concentrating on one's own advantage, pleasure, or well-being without regard for others."

The key words here are "without regard for others". Taking 30 minutes for a bubble bath; taking an art course; running; writing; reading; or dreaming - these activities are not without regard for others. They are not being concerned excessively with oneself – they are self-care.

My husband can tell when I have gone too long without taking some *Me Time*. I am snappy and irritable. It is also evident to me when he needs a break. *Me Time* does not just apply to Moms. It is something that everyone needs. As a family, we need to encourage each other to schedule our own *Me Time*.

By and large, mothers and housewives are the only workers who do not have regular time off. They are the great vacationless class. Anne Morrow Lindbergh

Finding Me Time

If you have done the exercises up to this point, you already have an idea of what *you* need to do. You may already be doing it. Have you started to research the night courses available towards your degree? Have you started to go to the gym twice a week? Are you taking lunch alone once a week? Have you added some of the activities from chapter two to your daily To-Do list?

If NOT it is time to start. As Mark Twain said, *"The secret of getting ahead is getting started. The secret of getting started is breaking your complex overwhelming tasks into small manageable tasks, and then starting on the first one."*

GETTING STARTED

1. REVIEW YOUR *Life Map* on page 42 to see if you can use one of these goals to assist with finding *Me Time*. Or you can just commit to the time – 15 minutes a day and decide what to do later.

2. START SMALL – it is okay to start with one activity per week or just a few minutes a day.

3. BOOK AN APPOINTMENT with yourself in your day-timer or family calendar.

4. CONGRATULATE YOURSELF on your successes and if you miss a day or miss a time don't fret over it. Just re-book your time.

What to Do with Your Time

Okay you have the time booked. What are you going to do? If you just spend the time thinking about what you think you should be doing (work or chores) or feel guilty that you should be with the kids, it won't help you. You need to focus on you, even for a few minutes. Activities will differ by the day and by your To Do list. Sometimes doing errands alone counts and other times you may need a bubble bath. Timing also can vary greatly. Some days you may have to grab the seconds while you can - when the kids are in a sports program or down for a nap. Other days you may have pre-booked a massage. And once in awhile you may need a full day or two.

See if this list can give you some ideas of things you can do:
- Sit in a dark room for one minute and just breathe
- Go to a museum
- When out running errands, stop for a coffee – no one will notice the extra 15 minutes
- Run errands to your favourite store by yourself
- When your husband and kids are playing, sneak in a 15-minute bubble bath
- Buy a *Chicken Soup for the Soul* book and read two stories a day
- Lock yourself in the bathroom

- Take a book into the kitchen with you and tell everyone you are cleaning - read first
- Leave the housework for one or two extra days and use that time for you
- Get up early and go for a walk
- Trade childcare with a friend or neighbour... this way you will both get some time off
- Join a book club
- Take a class or a course
- Surf the internet
- Try to get up 15 minutes before the kids
- Use hired help every so often
- Read for 15 minutes a day – alternate between fiction, non-fiction and magazines
- Exercise
- Start a craft project
- Work at a job you love
- Travel
- Make a quilt
- Meet a friend for lunch
- Commute with a friend
- Write a book
- Work in your garden
- Go for a bike ride
- Make a friend on the internet
- Go for coffee at 6:00 am and be home before the kids get up

- Write in a journal
- Play a musical instrument
- Watch a favourite TV show
- Take pictures
- Scrap book or work on photo albums
- Learn a new hobby
- Walk your dog

What is your hobby? Every woman ought to have some pet interest in life, outside of the everyday routine, which composes her regular occupations. What is yours?
The Mother's Magazine, January 1915, quote found in Simple Abundance, Sarah Ban Breathnach.

Activity

Your Commitment

I, _____, believe I deserve to take care of myself. I will make sure to take some time for me everyday. I will also make sure that I am aware that my family also needs *Me Time* and help them to find it.

ACTIVITIES I would like to include in my *Me Time* are:

Ways Moms are Finding Time Alone

Get up early or use your lunch hour, but if you forget about yourself, so will everyone else. *Jasmine*

When I am at the end of my rope, I go to my sister's for the weekend and then have a spa treatment or two. I find the peace and quiet (not to mention the uninterrupted sleep!) and time away is rejuvenating. *Leane*

I have a part time job that I absolutely love and it is my time out (and I get paid to do it!) *Kathy*

I stay up late and read. *Mom*

I disappear into the tub to do some product testing. *Paula, a creator of natural care products*

I lock myself in the basement to scrap book. *Wanda*

My husband and I each have one scheduled night a week to do our own thing. *Mom*

I put it in my palm pilot as an appointment. *Pat*

I take "mental health days" when I feel I need them. Dust bunnies will actually WAIT... Go Figure. Over time, I have learned that if I was not healthy, nothing went right; I realized it was critical to take self-care seriously. *Deb*

Tammy sums it all up for us; "You are the most important person in your life. If you love yourself enough to make that time for you, you will have lots of love to share in the rest of your life."

Sneaky Me Time

Okay, let's be totally realistic. I admit there will be times when **Me Time** is impossible to find, much less schedule. Of course, these will be days when we are desperate for it, so I say, "Let's be sneaky!" See if you can try a version of one of the suggestions below to sneak in some **Me Time.**

- Keep books on tape in the car with you. They can be novels, inspirational or even a new language. If you are in traffic or spending a few hours as a taxi Mom, turn it into **Me Time** by listening to a tape.

- Carry books, magazine articles, your journal or your favorite craft with you all the time. You can transform waiting time into **Me Time.**

- Adjust your attitude and enjoy doctor, dentist and other appointments. Find at least one positive in the experience - you are alone, you get to lie down, or you may be able to read! Although, I won't go as far as to say a root canal will be fun!

- Rather than run errands in a panic, rushing to get it over - enjoy what you are doing. Take five minutes to look through magazines, browse through the knick-knack store, or stop for a coffee.

- Finally, offer to do one of the family chores – clean up the kitchen, clean a bathroom, wash clothes – ALONE. Light your favorite candles, put on some music, and have a cup of tea or a glass of wine!

Being Creative

Some days, try as we might, we may not be able to get away and have time totally alone. On these days we need to be creative.

As I was writing this chapter, plans for a family trip were cancelled as my daughter was sick and we didn't feel she was up for an eight-hour car ride. My husband had a mountain bike race and so went alone.

He left on Friday morning and by that evening I was desperate for some time alone. After a week of my daughter being sick and my son being a three-year-old boy (that story could be another book!) along with the disappointment of not getting to go away, I felt off balance.

Since I was home alone with the kids, I couldn't very well go out so I convinced the kids that they needed to go play in the back yard. They agreed to 10 minutes, which led to one hour. I sat by myself, relaxed, and watched a TV show in peace. That hour grounded me for the weekend. The kids came in and we had a great weekend.

So what can you do if you are desperate for some **Me Time** and can't get away from your kids? See if some of these creative suggestions used by some work-at-home mothers would be suitable for your distressed moments:

Being Creative

Jennifer of, www.MyMommyBiz.com, has a small child size desk next to her own, outfitted with crayons, paper and even a keyboard. Her daughter stays occupied by copying Mom and working too.

Traci, an at-home childcare provider, survives the day by having quiet time in the afternoon. The little ones sleep and the older ones watch TV or read.

Alice, of www.CultureBridge.com, sets up "stations" at her kitchen table like they use in a preschool. Stations include puzzles, crafts, toys, computers, and snacks. On bad weather days she pulls the cars out of the garage and lets her children ride their bikes and scooters.

Natalie, of www.EnchantedEvents.ca, uses play dough and a play office (box filled with envelopes, used stamps & glue stick, paper, ballpoint pen, hole puncher, calculator) to entertain her children in a pinch.

Paula, of www.Mossberry.com, plans the workday's tasks to include her son. She will do shipping that day, as he loves to help stick labels, play with packing peanuts, and tape boxes.

Leane, who runs an auto repair shop, sets up a tent inside or outside, with sleeping bags, toys and snacks for her children to enjoy.

Carrie, a CPA, lets her son have a box of misprinted business cards and a box of envelopes to play with. When she is really desperate she has a stock of unopened cars that she can pull out and give to him.

Amanda, of AmandaMarks Business Solutions, sets up a special play area in her son's room (complete with the office phone to examine), and then retreats to her own room next door for 15 minutes of total relaxation.

Lynn, of www.WorkoutsForYou.com, uses her laptop to get work done in a variety of areas in the house. She can work when her daughter is snacking or watching TV and still be with her.

Christine, of www.CreativeKidsatHome.com, has a few containers filled with books, magazines, toys, puzzles, crafts or anything else new and unusual that she can pull out.

I have done a lot of work at restaurants with play areas. My kids play and I work. They think this is a treat! I have even had meetings there when no childcare was available.

Mom Management

No one will offer you this **Me Time**, you need to arrange it for yourself. Often all you need to do is ask! If you don't let your family know you need this time, it won't happen.

Ask, and it shall be given to you; seek, and ye shall find; knock, and it shall be opened unto you. Matthew 7:7

Being a mom is an amazing experience. The joy and happiness we receive is incredible, but it is not an easy job. To be the best mom for our children we need to be energized. As this chapter demonstrates, all Moms need **Me Time.** As we move into the next chapter we will take a look at what other areas we need to consider as we take care of ourselves. It is up to us to care for the Me in Mommeee so we can be the best Mommy for our children.

Motherhood brings as much joy as ever, but it still brings boredom, exhaustion, and sorrow too. Nothing else ever will make you as happy or as sad, as proud or as tired, for nothing is quite as hard as helping a person develop his own individuality-especially while you struggle to keep your own.
Marguerite Kelly and Elia Parsons

Taking Care of Me

Health, Nutrition and Spirit

TAKING CARE OF ME

How often do we walk out the door with our children well fed but forget about ourselves? How often do we cover our children with sunscreen only to let ourselves get burned? How often do we let our exercise program go because it interferes with a family member's schedule? How often do we stay up until the wee hours to get things done?

There is one more extremely important area we as Moms need to remember when managing our lives - we need to take care of ourselves physically. It is so easy for us to get caught up in the swing of life that we often forget our own health. We chose to ignore what our bodies are telling us. Even when we are taking time for us and we are realizing some of our dreams, if our body stops functioning, we won't be able to accomplish much.

Mom Management

Since there are so many incredible resources already available to us on health topics, I am going to keep this chapter fairly general. Regardless of our religious, cultural or personal beliefs, there are some basic principles that apply to the maintenance of good health. The first is knowledge. We need to make sure we know what we believe and what is important to us. We need to decide what feels right to us in regards to our health. This can fluctuate throughout our lives. Many people change their nutrition or exercise habits many times throughout their lives.

No matter what guidelines we follow or beliefs we have, *common sense* and *moderation* applies to us all. Listening to our bodies and using our common sense is a very strong component of healthy lifestyles. We all know when we need to be more active, get more sleep or stop snacking late at night. We now need to make sure we trust and follow these instincts.

Live by what you trust, Not by what you fear. Anonymous

Moderation... Many people live in extremes - they exercise excessively or not at all. They eat everything in sight or follow a restrictive diet. Moderation and balance work together. There needs to be a balance between the forbidden and the excessive. Our common sense is usually aware of this and can guide us to make the right choices.

If we could give every individual the right amount of nourishment and exercise, not too little and not too much, we would have found the safest way to health. Hippocrates

All I ask from you in this chapter is to practise personal awareness. Adjust the ideas in the following pages to your beliefs. Be honest with yourself so that you can make the right decisions. Listen to your common sense. There are many types of programs and care available and you need to make sure you are doing what feels right for you. Use the examples from other Moms, along with your own beliefs to guide you as you make your decision to take care of yourself.

There are two main components to taking care of me. You need to care for your health/body and your spirit.

Health/Body – this involves getting enough rest, relaxation, eating well, exercise, stretching, dental/doctor appointments, massages, etc.

Spirit – reading, writing, thinking, observing, learning, time alone, time with friends, time with partner, one on one time with family, etc.

HEALTH

He who enjoys good health is rich, though he knows it not.
Italian Proverb

We know what we need to do – we need to get enough sleep, eat well and exercise. The question is do we do it?

We need to take care of our bodies with regular visits to the doctor, dentist, optometrist, massage therapist, chiropractor, naturopath, as well as a variety of other health care providers. Depending on our age, there is a variety of preventative care and testing we need to be aware of – your doctor can let you know what types of testing is suitable for each age. We are all very proactive when making sure that our children visit their health care providers regularly. We need to treat ourselves as well as we treat our children.

I recently had to get a tetanus shot after accidentally walking into a fence and getting poked by metal. Did you know that it is recommended that everyone get a tetanus shot every 10 years? I didn't. I follow the vaccination guidelines for my children but never thought about myself.

Are you getting your check ups?

SLEEP

Health is the first muse, and sleep is the condition to produce it. Ralph Waldo Emerson

I love to sleep. After becoming a Mom, sleep becomes a truly precious commodity. There is nothing as wonderful as a new baby but getting up in the middle of the night to feed that precious child can be pure agony. Eventually we do establish a routine, but there are many sleep deprived mothers walking around. Even after our children get older, we find ourselves sacrificing our sleep to get things done. I have left many a job to do after my children were in bed or before they woke up in the morning.

Sleep, however, isn't a luxury but a necessity. Our bodies require sleep to function. Sleep deprived drivers are considered as dangerous as impaired drivers. Think about all the other activities we just float through when we are tired. When I am tired, food doesn't taste as good, I have less patience for my children and husband, and nothing is as enjoyable. We certainly can determine our children's mood by the amount of sleep they get, so we need to do this for ourselves.

According to James Maas, Ph. D., a professor of psychology at Cornell University, in Ithaca, New York, and author of *Power Sleep* (Harper Perennial, 1999), "The process of sleep, if given adequate time and the proper environment, provides tremendous power. It restores, rejuvenates, and energizes the body and brain. The third of your life that you should spend sleeping has profound effects on the other two thirds of your life, in terms of alertness, energy, mood, body weight, perception, memory, thinking, reaction time, productivity, performance, communication skills, creativity, safety, and good health."

With this expert advice in mind, use these tips to help you get a better sleep:

- Exercise early in the day
- Consume caffeine early in the day
- Use comfortable mattresses, pillows and sheets
- Keep your bedroom dark, cool and quiet
- Go to bed and get up at the same time every day
- Watch what you eat and drink before bed

NUTRITION

One should eat to live, not live to eat. Molière

Are you eating the right foods? Are you eating enough? Amazingly many women don't eat enough. "Women who eat irregularly, or only once a day have a slower rate of metabolism than women who eat regularly," said dietician Leslie Beck, at the Women's Health Matters Forum & Expo in Toronto. "The best way to boost your energy and your metabolism is to keep your blood sugar levels up by eating every five hours."

Take some time and look into nutrition – have a peek at the latest food guide, and be aware of what you are eating. Keep a food journal for a few days to see what you are really eating. Record everything, even that spoonful of peanut butter while making your children's lunch! Also record how you feel after eating certain foods. Do they affect your energy levels or moods? You will likely be surprised at your eating habits and can better make decisions.

Be aware of marketing where food and diet are concerned. I have read articles, books and media reports on almost every kind of food. There are so many contrasting studies. If you look hard enough you will find a study that cites the benefits of one food and another that says the same product is unhealthy.

Common sense and moderation are truly the keys to nutrition. We all know that we can't survive on junk food, but there is nothing wrong with eating pizza or chocolate once in awhile. If we are honest with ourselves and listen to our bodies, we know what we need to do and eat.

As one mother, Jasmine, puts it, "You have to eat, so why not make the right choice for your body. Do not deprive yourself and do indulge occasionally but balance the good with the bad."

Just trust yourself, then you will know how to live. Johann Wolfgang Von Goethe

---

Tips from Moms on Nutrition

Eat what you make for your kids. *Jan*

Cook double or triple batches and freeze the meals. *Christine*

Dinner always becomes lunch for the next day. *Mom*

I make 100 meatballs at a time and freeze them in batches of 20. *Lisa*

Use a crock-pot. *Maureen*

I try to fix meals with meat, vegetables or fruit and bread/rice twice a day. *Alice*

Fill your fridge with easy-to-reach healthy foods. *Amanda*

Never take teenage boys shopping with you. *Harwant*

Plan ahead. Sit down on Sunday and pick your meals for the week. *Mom*

Put supper in the oven and go for a quick run. Use bagged salad. *Harjeet*

EXERCISE

I love this quote…

The first time I see a jogger smiling, I'll consider it. Joan Rivers

Yes, we also have to exercise. In our world of modern conveniences, most of us do not get the physical activity we need from our general lifestyle. We need to find ways to incorporate it into our lives. Depending on the ages of our children, we may get some exercise just chasing them around, but in general we have to make an effort to add it to our daily schedule.

Physical activity has three main components:

Cardiovascular exercise – we need to get our heart pumping and lungs working.

Strength exercise – we need to do resistance exercises for the health of our bones and muscles.

Stretching exercises – we need to keep our muscles relaxed and our joints mobile.

According to Health Canada, "The benefits of regular activity include:

- Better health
- Improved fitness
- Better posture and balance

- Better self-esteem
- Weight control
- Stronger muscles and bones
- Feeling more energetic
- Relaxation and reduced stress
- Continued independent living in later life."

They go on to suggest that we, "Consider adding activity – more time, more effort, more often. If you are already regularly active, you can still benefit by adding activity. Generally, the more active you are, the more benefits you will get".

Physical activity doesn't just mean going to the gym. We need to fit in 30 to 60 minutes (depending on intensity) of activity daily. We can do it all at once or we can break it into 10-minute segments, spread throughout the day.

By varying the three components of exercise throughout our week, we are more likely to continue our activity. Just as we do not eat the same food at every meal, we should not do the same exercise for every workout. We can include lifestyle exercises like walking to work, taking the stairs, parking farther away from the door, gardening, house cleaning, or stretching while watching TV; or we can partake in traditional exercises such as running, biking, weight lifting, fitness classes, or team sports. Physical activity means moving… so lets get moving.

There are many more benefits to physical activity than just improved health. It is an excellent form of stress relief. There is nothing like a boxing class to relieve the stress of whining children. Exercise can provide us with **Me Time** or family time. We may enjoy couple time by playing tennis together. Exercise is also an excellent mood lifter. I have never been in a worse mood after a workout!

Tips from Moms on Fitness

Make it a family ritual – go for walks, hikes or skating. *Stephanie*

My husband and I alternate days to go to the gym. *Mom*

I use my stair climber whenever I watch TV. *Shannon*

Purchase exercise videos. *Maureen*

I get up ½ hour before everyone and get on the treadmill. I find that it really clears my head and prepares me for the day. *Hyla*

Use a gym that has childcare. Book your children in advance so you feel obligated to go. *Jeanette*

Walk to as many places as you can. *Pam*

SPIRIT

Another area to consider in taking care of ourselves is taking care of our spirit, and in essence this is what this book is about. By learning to listen to our dreams, set goals, balance our lives and take time for ourselves, we are truly caring for our spirit. Life is much more pleasurable when we are able to enjoy it. We will go through difficult periods in life. We will have hard decisions to make. We will have family issues, relationship issues, work issues and real life issues, but if we have developed strength in our mind and spirit we will be better equipped to deal with these issues.

When we are rested, healthy, in shape, and have a strong spirit, we will experience great joy in our lives. We will be able to build strong, healthy and happy families.

We now move into a new section of this book. Having taken the journey to true Mom Management, we must include a few skill sets that, we as Mom Managers need in order to run the business of family. We cannot truly be taking care of ourselves unless we are also caring for our loved ones. The first of these skill sets is shifting our views on time and looking at it as a gift.

The Gift of Time
Shift Your Perspective

God could not be everywhere and therefore he made mothers.
Jewish proverb

If there were a description for the job of Mother, it would surely list time management and organization as two of the most important skills necessary. Becoming a Mom means that we not only have to deal with our own things but we also have to do it for the rest of our family. Now that we have learned the importance of caring for the Me in Mommeee, we need to make sure we have our time and organization skills fine-tuned.

TIME MANAGEMENT

Time management... what a catch phrase. We don't need to manage our time; we need more of it. In fact, every survey that was returned for this book indicated a lack of time as a major stressor. Unfortunately, we just can't have more time. There are only 86,400 seconds in each day and that is not going to change. What needs to change is how we view and manage our time.

You will never find time for anything. If you want time you must make it. Charles Buxton

THE GIFT OF TIME

As I grow older, I see time as a gift. I see how fast it goes and I make every attempt to cherish it. It seems like yesterday that I found out I was pregnant and now my daughter is in grade one. It won't be long before I am reading this chapter and laughing as my son (who is now four) is heading off to university. We certainly can't control the speed of time but we can control what we do with it. Rather than just let it pass us by, we can take advantage of it and enjoy it. In essence, this entire book is about our time. *Mom Management* is about how we manage our lives and the decisions we need to make. As I have heard Oprah Winfrey say, "You are the manager of your life."

Before we can begin to look at the tools and skills of time management, we have to look at where we are at now and gain an understanding of what we expect to accomplish by managing our time.

When you arise in the morning, think of what a precious privilege it is to be alive -- to breathe, to think, to enjoy, to love. Marcus Aurelius

Shifting Our Perspective

The first step in gaining control over our time is to *shift our perspective*. We really only have two choices:

We can complain about all the time we don't have.

OR

We can learn to respect, appreciate and be thankful for the time we do have.

I have made the second choice. I make a conscious effort to be thankful for the time I have and to respect it. Through this respect, I have learned to be aware of what goes on around me. Of course, I still go through periods where I am busy and overwhelmed but I can deal with those because I understand why they are happening. I then make sure they are balanced with periods of calm. During the times of overload, if I stop and think about why I am so busy it makes a huge difference to my perspective.

Last Christmas was a very busy time for me. Rather than letting it be stressful, I found it exciting. It meant that my business was where it needed to be. I was busy because I was

119

successful. I also knew that in January things would slow down and I would have time to recover.

In our hectic society, it can be very difficult to avoid busyness. Things seem to come in chunks – you will have five things one weekend and none the next. When we feel weighed down by what is going on around us, it is time to *stop, look and listen*.

Stop, Look and Listen

If we can remember this familiar saying, we have provided ourselves with a tool to *Shift our Perspective*. When we find ourselves feeling like we are out of control of our time; feeling busy and overwhelmed, or we don't seem busy but still can't get anything done, we need to Stop, Look, and Listen.

STOP – STOP either physically or mentally.

LOOK – Take notice of what you are doing and why you are busy. Take time to think about why you are doing the things that are making you busy. What is motivating you to do so much that you are overwhelmed?

LISTEN – Listen to your instinct and common sense. Are you doing things that lead to your priorities or those of your family? Are you doing things that are important to you? Does it feel right? Can you see this time as a gift or do you need to change how you are using this time? Sometimes, even during craziness, we can see that what we are doing is very important and can be considered as a *gift* of time. We usually can also see an end to the craziness. If, however, we can't connect the activities to our priorities or see a real why for what we are doing, it is time to change our behavior.

In order for this method to work, we have to make sure we have a framework in place. We need to understand our pressure points and our priorities.

Our Pressure Points

We need to learn to be aware of our pressure points – the situations where we feel very stressed over a lack of time. There is a difference between being crazy busy *just because* or being crazy busy for a reason. When we know our priorities and dreams, they can motivate us through our very busy periods. We can deal with great demands on our time if we understand why we are doing what we are doing or what we will achieve. We can support our family through similar times if we know they are following their goals and dreams. However, we cannot continue to keep up with this hectic pace for unlimited periods of time.

Mom Management

We all have a pressure point, where we are doing too much and can't maintain the pace. It differs between people and at different times of our lives. We need to make sure we are aware of our personal limits and notice as they start to change. As mothers we are likely aware of our children's limits, but are we aware of our own? I react differently to similar events now than I did when I was in my 20s. My Mom, a retired teacher, can't imagine how I can handle my current lifestyle. Yet, she remembers doing it herself and it seemed normal.

Some of the signs we are doing too much include:

Sickness	Stress	Negative attitude
Tiredness	Moodiness	Lack of enthusiasm

Activity

What is your pressure point? When do you start to sense you are doing too much? What are your signs?

What do you do when you see this point coming?

Down Time

In order to stay sane and in control of our lives we need to mix our busy periods with variety and alternate them with downtime. When we are busy, we need to make sure it is with a selection of things – a mix of the fun, the difficult and the necessary. Busy can include family activities, our careers, sports, life maintenance activities, and our personal goals and dreams. Downtime can include relaxation activities, family time, reading, exercise, yoga, sleep, nature walks, or doing nothing at all.

You must have been warned against letting the golden hours slip by. Yes, but some of them are golden only because we let them slip. J.M. Barrie

Many of my most inspirational ideas come when I slow down. Often it is when I am laying in bed at night. The house is quiet, I am quiet, and my mind is able to create. I have nothing to distract my thought process and it is amazing the ideas that come to me. I keep paper by the bed to try to jot ideas down. I visualize and work through my dreams and my goals. Now, if I do this too often it interferes with my sleep!

Listen to Our Body

When we don't have these calm periods to relax and recuperate, we chance pushing our body beyond its limits. We need to listen to our bodies. If, as we covered in chapter seven, we do not take care of ourselves – physically and mentally, we chance total burnout

---

These are important lessons for our children to learn as well. We need to allow and encourage them to listen to their bodies. We need to help them discover their pressure points and to discover solutions to them. We need to encourage them to include quiet and recovery time in their schedules. We need to allow them a chance to let their creativity bloom. At the end of a school day, a sports tournament, a busy weekend, a stressful situation, or a week of exams, we need to support our children and partners need for downtime.

Do you know how we teach our children these lessons? **We do it ourselves. If they see us living our lives this way, they will learn from example.**

Activity

What do you like to do for downtime? Can you use this as your **Me Time**?

Do you encourage your family to partake in downtime – both individually and as a family?

How can I remember to stop and ask myself WHY when I am busy and overwhelmed?

What will I do if my WHY isn't a very good reason?

We can learn to live with time as our enemy or our partner. Making the most effective use of time is a conscious decision. We need to *stop, look and listen*. Once we have made the decision, we need to work at it and we need to remind ourselves of it often. We need to work on time management as a family. We need to respect each other's priorities. We need to value time and use it as our ally.

> One of my favorite books on Time Management is *How to Get Control of Your Time and Your Life* by Alan Lakein, Signet Books. After seeing this book quoted in almost every other book I have read on the subject, I figured I should read it too! It is full of excellent ideas and information.

Time is a Gift. Cherish it. Be Thankful for it. Tracy Lyn
Moland

Choose A Reminder

In order to stay in control of this shift in perspective, choose a reminder to keep you on track. Pick something that happens fairly regularly during your day – the phone, the dog barking, the hourly beep on your watch, the kids saying Mom, or an email coming in.

Every time you hear this sound, use it as your reminder to check in on your perspective of time. Are you feeling like you don't have enough time or are you feeling lucky that you have these opportunities?

If the kids are whining and you wish the day was over, *shift your perspective* and be happy that you are able to be home with them.

Do you have overlapping work projects? Be thankful that you are working at a job you love.

Are you tired of spending all your time cleaning your house? Look around at the house you were so excited to buy.

Are you enjoying the TV show you are watching? Or are you using it to avoid something else?

IDENTIFY YOUR PRIORITIES

In chapters two through five, the activities we did helped us to determine our life priorities. Determining these priorities is a major step towards taking control of our time.

By implementing these priorities into our day-to-day life, we use them as a guide. They guide us to make the best decisions to manage our time on our terms. We also need to think about those around us as we create our plans. The priorities of our family are very important to us, but being part of a family also includes compromise. There will be times when we need to hold off on one of our dreams because it conflicts with one of our partner or children's dreams. But we also need to make sure that they do the same for us. Many Moms will let their dreams go to put their families first, and that is why I wrote this book - *we need* to take care of ourselves.

If you want to make good use of your time, you've got to know what's most important and then give it all you've got.
Lee Iacocca

Activity:

Glance back at chapters two through six and have a look at what you have determined are your priorities. From this information answer the following questions.

Three of the goals I set for myself are (page 42):

The three to five main roles I want to focus upon in my life are (page 53):

For each of these priorities you have determined (goals and roles), write down or think about WHY they are priorities. These are the *whys* you will use to motivate you to do these things.

When we are pursuing our own dreams, we teach our children to do the same. If we continually put our life and dreams on hold for them, then they will expect to do the same when they are adults. They will learn that dreaming is only for children. If we respect our dreams, our children will do the same.

Shifting our perspective and understanding our priorities is the key to effectively managing our time, but once we understand this, there are time management tools that are incredibly helpful if we implement them. The next chapter will cover some of the systems and tools that I have both learned to use, and found to be most effective as a Mother.

Tools of The Trade
Effective Systems

EFFECTIVE SYSTEMS TO ORGANIZE OUR TIME

The next step after determining our priorities is to create a plan and use effective systems to execute the plan. By systems, I refer to the methods we use to manage our activities and schedules. It can be planners, reminder systems or check lists. There is just no way to keep track of the many activities we juggle in life without first formalizing a system we will use.

Life offers two great gifts--time, and the ability to choose how we spend it. Planning is a process of choosing among those many options. If we do not choose to plan, then we choose to have others plan for us. Richard I. Winword

As Moms, we already have a number of these types of systems in place. We each have our own, unique way of keeping things sane in our families. At this point, it is extremely important for us to identify the systems we are currently using. We then need to determine which ones work for us, which ones work when we use them, and then *use them consistently*. Managing time never comes easy, but if we are consistent with what works for us, we can do it.

Activity

What systems do I use to manage my time?

Are they working?

What are systems that would work if you used them?

Common Sense

We used our common sense when implementing a strategy to take care of ourselves physically. It is again a powerful tool to assist with our time management strategy.

For example, if I need to be somewhere early in the morning, I know I can't turn my computer on. If I do I will end up frustrated as I rush to get the kids out the door, and I likely will be late.

Common sense is the knack of seeing things as they are, and doing things as they ought to be done. Josh Billings

Once we have determined what works for us, we all have to make the effort to use these methods and systems. There are many books, articles, seminars, and speakers on the subject because we constantly need to remind ourselves to stay on track. We need to *DO* what works for us.

Even as an "*expert*" in the field, I have been late or have missed something. I know exactly why it happens; I have fallen off my system. I haven't been faithful to my planner - I didn't write an appointment in or worse, I wrote it in but didn't check my schedule. Staying in control of your time as a Mom is definitely challenging but it is something we need to do and can do.

Activity

Do I already know what works and what I need to do to manage my time?

Is there one thing I could do that I know would make the difference in managing my time?

Once we know what is working and not working in managing our time, we are ready to look at new ideas and see what things we can add or change.

THE TOOLS

There are certain things that make it easier to manage our time. But they only work if we use them so make sure to choose a method that fits you and your lifestyle.

1. Choose **ONE** main CALENDAR or PLANNER for the family. More than one can mean overlapping and missed events. (Now it is okay to have a back up. My planner is the main one and absolutely everything goes into it but I also have a wall calendar in the bathroom that I put things on for easy viewing and reminders). With older children, each family member will need their own system and calendar, but in order for you, as Mom, to stay sane, there needs to be one main system and that needs to be yours.

2. CHOOSE a system that appeals to you and your preferences. The two main types are paper and electronic/computer.

Paper – the possibilities are endless. Spend some time finding one that really appeals to YOU. Questions to help you decide:

Do I like to add/remove items? (Go with a binder style)

Do I want it to be portable?

Do I like to have themes, styles, inspirational notes or would I prefer to keep it plain?

Will I use all the components of it? If not, can I remove them?

Will it fit in my purse/diaper bag/brief case?

What have I used before?

What did I like/dislike about it?

Electronic:

Do I need something that I can carry with me?

Is it compatible with my current system?

Do I have the option to use or remove different features?

Do I want it to be compatible with my phone?

Do I like how it operates?

Start Slowly – Only implement one or two new ideas at a time. If you try to change everything, you will only add to your feeling of being overwhelmed.

3. Use this main planner FOR *EVERYTHING* – including your work, appointments, family's activities, exercise, and most importantly, your **Me Time**.

4. MATCH the size to your lifestyle. My retired mother-in-law uses a small calendar with an entire month on each page. I need at least one full page per day. If you are on the go, make sure it is portable. A big wall calendar doesn't help when you are at hockey practice or in the office.

5. The COMPONENTS of your system will vary by preference but there are a few necessary components:

   - Yearly calendar
   - Monthly calendar
   - A page for each day (or a lot of writing room)
   - Room for notes/lists
   - Your **To Do** list – which deserves its own section below.
   - Your goals and dreams. List your priorities in your planner. At the beginning of each day review your goals and make sure that you are doing something to work toward them. Each month review your long-term goals, alter your short-term goals, or add new goals.

6. PERSONALIZE Your System. Now depending on your lifestyle there are lots of different components/options that you may want to include in your system.

- Phone List/Phone log
- Family Budget
- Expense Reports
- Travel/car logs
- Emergency Contacts
- Medical Information
- Grocery Lists —a standard one that you always use
- Assignment lists
- Fitness Journal

My favorite agenda is Jenny Hoops', *The Road to Excellence* (www.jennyhoops.com). It is filled with inspirational writing and quotes and provides excellent goal-setting guidelines.

TO DO LISTS

Aaaaaagh, those darned To Do lists! Do we have to discuss them; do we have to have them? Do they really work?

Remember way back when? At some point during our schooling we learned study skills. Guess what? We received our first class in time management. A study skills program starts with effective use of a day timer or planner – and many schools provide students with these.

If we as Moms use the skills our children are learning, we can stay in control. If we encourage our children to take advantage of what they are learning, and help them to properly use their planners, they will develop a life lasting habit. Rather than having to find and take time management courses as adults, they will have already acquired the skills.

If your children have received a planner from school, take a few minutes and go through it. You will find a lot of advice that you can apply to your life and your planning system.

Activity

Grab a piece of paper and quickly write out your current To Do list.

Have you ever thought of something you had to remember while driving or in the middle of the night? In order to remember it, we repeat it over-and-over to ourselves. We probably don't sleep that well because it is on our mind. Sometimes we play games with ourselves. I will switch my wedding ring to my right hand to help me remember something. It usually works. Often we drive ourselves crazy trying to remember that *one thing* and still forget it. Now take that one thing and multiply it by the 10 or 20 things we have to remember. Our mind spins like a merry go round and a few things are going to fly off!

How a To Do List Should Work

Using grocery shopping as an example, let's see why To Do lists work. When I go shopping with a specific list that is well planned out and is based around meals for the week (like the ones in *Cooking for the Rushed*), I stick very close to the list. I still buy the odd item not on my list – grocery stores spend a lot of money to attract impulse purchases, but not much more. Without a list, I have spent $80.00 on milk (milk along with all the other things I thought I needed), plus I always forget at least one item. Shopping is definitely less stressful when we have a plan.

To Do lists do the same thing for our lives. They allow us to pull things out of our head and put them on paper, freeing our mind to live. They allow us to keep track of what we are doing, need to do, or have completed. They also can help prevent procrastination – when the same item appears day after day after day, we realize we either need to do it or forget it.

Mom Management

Each of us has our own way of creating and using a To Do list, but there are definite things we need to keep in mind, if we want to create an *effective* list.

1. Use ONE list for all tasks.
2. Use your PLANNER/COIL BOOK so you can't lose the list and if you need to refer back to something you know where to look.
3. PLAN for 10 MINUTES at the same time EVERY DAY, preferably in the morning or evening in a quiet place.
4. REVIEW YOUR DREAMS and GOALS daily and make sure they are part of your list.
5. TRANSFER UNFINISHED ITEMS that are still priorities from your last list and ADD new ones.
6. ADD NEW ITEMS as they arise.

Once you have completed your initial list, the following activity is crucial:

Activity

Grab the list you wrote up earlier in the chapter or go get today's list and do these steps to see how they work.

1. REVIEW your list and see what you can DELEGATE.
   Can you write someone's name next to something on your list? Can your partner or children do a task? Can your

assistant at work do it? Can you hire someone to do it? It is amazing the number of services that are available. Visit www.iceaweb.org for a listing of personal assistants that can do almost anything you need and usually for a very reasonable fee. For more information on delegating, refer back to chapter five.

2. REMOVE ITEMS from your list.

Do you really need to do all the things on your list? Will life continue on without doing a few of the items? Can you get by on the groceries in the house or put off vacuuming for a few days? Do you really need to go somewhere or can you make a phone call? Are you over-committed? Is it time to say no? Do the items on your list lead you in the direction you want to go?

3. PRIORITIZE YOUR LIST. This step is what makes To Do lists work.

We do not just randomly put things on our To Do lists. We put things there that we feel need to be done, but as we all know, we rarely get our lists accomplished. We need to alter how we look at our lists - it is not supposed to be a competition in which the person who does the most wins. If we are thinking this way, then we will consciously only put the things we know we can do on our lists. As I have stated above, we need to shift our perspective and we need to do what is truly important to us.

139

> Your top priorities should always be things that lead towards both your and your family's dreams and goals. When there are other things on your list, ask yourself if it is worth taking time away from your priorities in order to do these items, if the answer is 'Yes', do them. If it is 'No', then you need to remove them from your list.
>
> For example, cleaning may not lead to any of your goals and dreams, but at some point we do have to take the time to clean our homes.

We need to know what our priorities are to act on them, but they're not priorities unless we act on them. Kathy Peel

After writing our list and then going through it to delegate and remove items, we have to take one more step. We have to decide, based on what is going on right now in our lives, what are our true priorities. We then have to do our list in an order based upon these current priorities.

Choosing What's Most Important

I realize that this step sounds overwhelming. It is not meant to be; rather it is meant to make sure we aren't wasting our time and then complaining about it. Look at the whole picture as you pick your priorities. What is most important for your goals and dreams? What is most important for your family? What matters most? What is coming up in your schedule? These are the important things and the things you need to do first. If you are having a birthday party in two days, cleaning the bathroom may be a priority. If it is test time at school, chores may rank low on the list. If you have a work deadline coming up, it may not be the night for a gourmet dinner. If you are having trouble deciding on priorities, think about why you are doing something. Go through your list and use a priority classification such as the ones below.

Susan, a mother of three, numbers her list in order of importance. Paula, a work at home Mom, divides her list into MUST DO and SHOULD DO. Some people put stars or circles by the three to five most important things. Franklin/Covey, as well as Lakein, use a system of letters and numbers. A-1 is a top priority and C is low priority. Pick a system that works for you.

Once you have written your original list and followed the steps above of reviewing it, delegating, removing items and prioritizing what is left, it is time to DO YOUR LIST. Make sure to do it in your prioritized order while being flexible enough to make changes as the day goes on.

EFFECTIVENESS versus EFFICIENCY

Something we need to consider as we go through life with these long To Do lists – are we putting the right things on them? Are we doing the right job?

I was driving in my car listening to a tape on time management and I heard one of the most profound statements I have ever heard. Mathew Parvis stated the difference between Effectiveness and Efficiency.

Efficiency *is doing the job right.* Effectiveness *is doing the RIGHT job.* Be **effective** *first.* Mathew Parvis

You may need to think this one through a bit. We often spend a lot of time doing something right when we shouldn't even be doing it at all. I remember during university, I was cleaning my bathroom very efficiently. I even found a contact lens that someone else had lost – before I moved in two years earlier. However, I had final exams the next day. I was not making effective use of my time. Effective use would have been to study.

Think about how often you spend a lot of time doing something well when you should be doing something else. We, as Mothers often do this. "Oh, I just have to get the dishes done and then I will play." Or "I have to finish this and then we can go to the park." We get annoyed at our children for interrupting us doing a menial job, when the effective use of our time is likely to enjoy our children before they grow up. This doesn't mean we should live in a messy house but it does mean we need to ask ourselves this question every so often: "Am I being Effective first? Am I doing the *right* job?"

This question has really made a difference in my relationship with my children and my husband. I have made the decision to use my time as effectively as possible. Rather than always trying to get work done when they are around and want to be with me, I have made use of childcare and school to make sure to have effective time both for my work and for my family. When the kids are away, I work on my writing and presentations. When they are home I set aside time to play, go for walks or just *be* with them.

Of course, sometimes being effective is being able to multi-task. As a Mom we truly can't survive without this skill. I may cook supper while my children are doing homework or answer a few emails while they are watching TV. As we touched on in chapter four, we need to be aware of the times when we can't do this as well.

Being effective can relate to many areas of our lives. My husband and I try to find quality time alone together a few times a month. On our recent trip to Mexico, it was just amazing to be a couple again. We laughed, played and talked. Rather than finding ourselves talking family all the time, we were able to strengthen our relationship while laughing on a kayak. Being aware of the difference between the two has helped me to improve both the quality of my work and my relationships.

Here are some areas of our lives that benefit from making sure we are being effective and doing the right job:

Chores – When we do them and how much time we spend doing them. Do we need to vacuum everyday?

Family time – Are we really being together as a family? There is a difference between watching TV together and a family night.

Work – Can we focus on work so we can leave it there when we are done?

Relationships – We need to spend quality time with our family and friends. My Dad and I email each other a lot but we both sure enjoy when he is in town and we can spend quality time together (he lives in Singapore).

Travel – Can we travel and leave work or our commitments behind?

Relaxing activities - Are we doing what we enjoy? Yes it is okay to watch our favorite TV shows, but do we need to watch hours of nothing? When we decide to relax, can we stop thinking about all that we have to do? (Moms, I know we are all guilty of this one!)

Now, when we are doing the right job, let's be efficient and make sure we do it well (not perfect!). If you ever feel like you are lost or working hard and getting nothing done, stop and consider if you are being efficient or effective.

ON THE RIGHT TRACK

As we finish these chapters on time, keep these four questions in mind to help you stay on track and effectively manage your time.

- If I Stop, Look and Listen at how I am using my time, can I consider it *The Gift of Time* or a waste of time?
- Can I *Shift my Perspective* and my perception of the time?
- Am I aware of my priorities? Does what I am doing lead to my priorities? If not, is it worth doing?
- Am I doing the right job?

The final skill set that we need as Mom Managers is that of organization, which we will cover in the final chapter of this book. Again, we each have our own comfort levels but in order to get maintain a house, we have to have some sort of organization!

Now is the only time there is. Make your now wow, your minutes miracles, and your days pay. Your life will have been magnificently lived and invested, and when you die you will have made a difference. Mark Victor Hansen

---

Time Saving Strategies from Moms

Use on-line grocery shopping. *Helen*

Try to do a few things at the same time. *Pam*

Keep organized. *Linda*

Use a list. *This was a very popular suggestion.*

Have enough underwear and towels to last two weeks!

Use meal plans. *Mom*

Cook in bulk. *Jasmine*

Use salad in a bag. *Harjeet*

Use a cleaning lady. *(Lots of Moms)*

Pre-cook parts of meals. (Cook and freeze ground beef)

Do as many errands as you can while you are out. *Helene*

Stay on top of things. *Christina*

Delegate chores to your children. *Patrice*

I keep my diaper bag packed and ready to go at all times. *Elouise*

Get things ready the night before. *Christine*

Keep lists posted in the kitchen so the family stays focused without being badgered. *Shannon*

Install and use a key rack at the door. *Alice*

***Authors note… USE is the key word!

Do errands alone! *Maureen*

Prioritize your life. *Adrianna*

Use a cordless phone and a headset. *Vicki*

Where Are My Keys?
Organization

MOM, WHERE IS MY...?

To round out this final section on skills, we will carefully consider the essential skill of organization. Lack of organization rated very high on the surveys as one of Moms major sources of frustration. No matter how much we wish we didn't have to deal with it, being organized is one of the most important skill sets for Mothers to have.

Now before I scare you, I need to clarify a bit - I am not talking about perfect, show home quality homes with everything in place, labelled and looking perfect. What I am talking about is being able to find your keys (you've probably noticed by now that this is a recurring event in my house); knowing where your children's books are on library day, or knowing how to deal with all your mail.

Out of clutter, find simplicity. Albert Einstein

I will keep this chapter fairly straightforward, as we will only consider the key points of organization. For further ideas, there are some wonderful books to read on this topic though you may need to check out a few to find one that matches with your style of organization. One that I suggest reading is, *Organizing from the Inside Out* by Julie Morgenstern, (Owl Books).

My organization advice is simple but effective. It comes down to three concepts – learn what works for you, limit how much you have, and make sure you have a home for what you have.

As we start, let's read Julie Morgenstern's new definition of organization and keep this in mind throughout the chapter: *"Organizing is the process by which we create environments that enable us to live, work, and relax exactly as we want to. When we are organized, our homes, offices, and schedules reflect and encourage who we are, what we want, and where we are going."* Recently Julie and her daughter were on TV and explained how even though their organizing styles may differ, they are both effective. We need to determine what works for us and for our families.

What Drives You Crazy?

This is a key point. We each have our organization limits. In workshops I teach on organization, I see some very diverse viewpoints. Some people are not bothered at all by clutter as long as they know where things are, whereas others need to have things color coordinated. Some people feel better in a home with a lot of clear, empty space and others love to be surrounded by a variety of things. We each have our breaking point where organization (or lack of it) is concerned – the one thing we can't stand and we need to be aware of it. If something doesn't bother us, then we shouldn't spend a lot of time organizing it or worrying about it. If something does bother us, then we need to deal with it and then let it go.

Activity

> Do these exercises as a family! Sometimes awareness is all we need to make changes.

1. WHAT IS YOUR *BREAKING POINT* WHEN IT COMES TO ORGANIZATION? What areas of your house or office frustrate you? What items can you never find? Set a timer for at least three minutes and list all the things that really drive you crazy. Include places, items, and people (yes, for now you can list the things that others in the family do!).

2. Now, GO BACK THROUGH THIS LIST AND THINK ABOUT WHY THESE THINGS BOTHER YOU. Using a scale of one to five (five being most important) determine how important these things are to your life. One of my main frustrations is a cluttered kitchen counter; I like to have it clear. The kitchen feels

open and airy, and it is easier to cook. Now on the scale, I rate this as a four in importance. If every time I have to cook, I need to clean things off it takes longer to cook and I am discouraged to start. If I just push things to the side it is easier for them to get lost or ruined. My daughter's bedroom is another area of frustration for me, but I only rate that as a two. She loves being able to walk in and have her toys ready to go. If she compromises and is willing to keep it clean and her clothes put away, I am willing to let her keep the toys out.

Take some time to look at your rating of items. You should begin to pinpoint some things that really do matter and others that are a waste of your time and energy. Parents of teenagers seem to agree that at some point you just learn to close the door and not worry about the state of the teen's bedroom.

I like to have a junk drawer. It used to drive me crazy and I always felt like I needed to organize it. I now realize it is better to have my coupons, my slips of paper, and my odds-and-ends all together. Even if it looks messy when I open it, I know exactly where to look for that *thing* when I finally realize what it is for. I used to spend hours trying to get it all organized, never finding the right place for the items, only to discover that the junk would re-accumulate.

<u>Activity</u>

Based upon your ratings, choose THREE THINGS you are willing to let go, that just aren't worth the time and energy you give them.

1.

2.

3.

And choose THREE THINGS you definitely want to have organized.

1.

2.

3.

Now that we have let our frustrations out, let's take a look at our life and see what works.

What Works for You?

Set the timer for five minutes and LIST all the things that *work for you* and your family. (For example, I never lose my keys, my kitchen is easy to cook in, my bedroom is comfortable, the kids have an effective tidy-up routine, I always walk out the door on schedule, etc.)

Congratulate yourself on this list. No one is totally hopeless at organization. I had a client whose organization skills were among the worst I have ever seen yet, he was able to function and knew his priorities. He knew where his skills were lacking and arranged to have these areas taken care of by hiring people to do them.

Activity

Take another five minutes and REVIEW your list of what works. Start another list along the side, listing the skills you now realize that you are using, that make these things work.

Are you always on time because you are good at preparing things the night before? Is your kitchen fairly organized because you have places for everything and you put things away? Is your bedroom organized because you limit how much stuff you keep in there? Is your closet efficient because you have an organizer? Is the house tidy because you have a family ritual of tidying for five minutes before bed?

Apply What Works to What Doesn't

Now we need to see if we can apply your list of what is working to your list of what is not working!

Can you apply what works in your bedroom to what drives you crazy in the kitchen? If you are never late for work but always late for social occasions, can you transfer your getting ready for work ritual to your getting ready to go out ritual? If one area is tidy because the family works together, can you apply this to another area?

Activity

I can use my skills at _____ (what works) to help me with _____ (what doesn't work).

Over the next couple of days, continually add to these lists. Come back to them when you find things that do work or things that drive you crazy. Try transferring the skills of one to the other.

Ask yourself *Why?* Why do you want to be organized, why do you want a room, a drawer, a car, a house, a yard, an activity, etc organized? Really listen to your answer.

Is it for you? Or is it for someone else? Are you doing what works for you and your family or what your own Mother would have expected?

Remember the discussion on Perfectionism in chapter five. Are you aiming to be perfectly organized or functionally organized?

Organization As A Family

We also need to find compromise within our family in our organizational efforts. There are things we need to learn to live with, things we need to insist on and things we need to do in respect to those around us. A family meeting is a great way to get this out in the open. As a family, go through the exercises above. Complete each section individually and then as a group.

When determining what works and what doesn't, also look at conflicting concerns. If something affects more than one family member, a compromise must be reached.

Often just sharing concerns at a meeting like this will solve a number of issues. When one family member becomes aware that something bothers another they will likely make the effort to move it, put it away, or change their habit. The importance of this family meeting is to agree to respect each other's opinion, and to agree that some things just need to be let go.

We need to know what works for our family but we also need to live. Don't let clutter or disorganization take over your life.

ORGANIZING PRINCIPLES

One never notices what has been done; one can only see what remains to be done. Marie Curie

Now that you have taken the time to determine what is working and what isn't working, see if some of the suggestions below will help you in your organizing quest. These are some basic principles that can be applied to the different areas in your life.

Organizing Basics

1. *Don't buy the organizing tools first.* Now this is a difficult one for me. I love Ikea® (www.ikea.com) and there is nothing more exciting than a trip there for organizing tools. Ok, the teacher in me is coming out; a trip to an office supply store is almost as exciting. I also love pens and paper, and of course, they have some neat organizing stuff there too! If we don't use the questions below that lead us to look at the stuff we have and where we currently keep it, storage systems won't help us. Storage tools are awesome but we need to use them

for the right things and in the right places. We don't want to end up with organizers for our storage tools!

2. *You can't do it all in one sitting or one day.* If you try to do too much you will become frustrated and not do anything at all. Pick one room to start and then pick one part of the room.

3. *Complete whatever you start* (so remember number two and start small).

4. *Give yourself enough time to do what you start.* (Although if you find you have a little pocket of time, pick a drawer or your purse or the diaper bag and just do that).

5. *DON'T organize areas unless they bother you.* If you can live with it, live with it. If the system works, don't change it!

6. *It will get messier before it is organized.* You will need to pull everything out and go through it. Again, this is another reason to do small sections. Once everything is out, divide it into four labelled boxes:

   - **Keep**
   - **Give Away**
   - **Throw Away**
   - **Decide Later** Put this box away and pull it out in six months. If you didn't miss it, give it away. If you did, start to use it again. If you still aren't sure, pack it up again.

Once everything is sorted, do as the labels on the boxes indicate, and either move on to another, small section or stop for the day

156

7. Once you are at this point and you have sorted and gotten rid of things, you can start to look at where you are putting your belongings. You may be pleasantly surprised at all the space you now have and will begin to see ways you can effectively use the space. Now may be the time to go to the store for some storage shelves, boxes or racks! Be creative and purchase pen and paper holders for your desk or dividers for your drawers. Choose the best organizing tools to make the area most effective.

As we continue on, you will find more detailed ideas and suggestions on how to deal with the things you pull out, as well as ways to prevent the clutter in the first place.

Limit How Much Stuff You Have

In today's society, there are so many things that we believe we need to have. We are constantly in search of new material things. Following are some ideas of ways to deal with some of the stuff in your life. These are excellent skills to teach our children (and our partners!).

Items – clothing, toys, household items, office supplies, etc. When the opportunity arises to add to our collections, take the time to ask yourself a few questions:

- Is this a REPEAT or SIMILAR to what we already have?

- Where will I put this item?
- What can I get rid of to make room for this new item? At our house during Christmas, my children put together a bag of give away toys that Santa takes in exchange for new toys.
- Wait a day or two to make a purchase. This will help to eliminate impulse purchases.

Every so often, go through the stuff you currently have and ask the following questions:

- How often do I use or wear this item?
- Does it still fit?
- Do I actually like this item?
- Why am I keeping it?
- Has the item expired, worn out, or stopped working?
- For books and magazines, will I read or refer to them again?
- Have my tastes changed?
- If it is sentimental, but I don't love it, can I keep the memory without the item?
- Do I use it? Do I want it?
- Do I want to continue to clean or maintain it?

Paper Products – flyers, magazines, newspapers, mail, letters, bills, school notes, invitations, announcements, etc.

DEAL with paper IMMEDIATELY and try to touch it only once.

- Read mail at your mailbox and then recycle it
- Record important dates, phone numbers, activities, events in your day-timer and recycle the item
- Tear out the articles you want to read from a newspaper or magazine and give it away or recycle it
- If it must be kept, file it immediately.

File items for retrieval, not for storage. It is better to have fewer, thicker folders than many specific ones. Use general and broad titles. You should know where to look quickly, even if it takes a few minutes to go through the papers. If your titles are too specific, you may have to go through many folders to find items.

Life is not a having and getting but a being and doing.
Unknown

Things Need A Home

Now that you have determined what you need and what drives you crazy, you need to make sure you have a place to put the items you want to keep. It doesn't really matter how many dolls my daughter has if she has somewhere to put them. It is when I find them all over the house that it drives me crazy.

There is no right or wrong about organization. We each have our own systems that work for us. The problem often is that we haven't figured out our system. A good rule of thumb – if it takes longer than a minute to know where something is, then it isn't in a good place. Notice I say, "to know where something is" rather than "to find it." I know where all my warranties and receipts are for household items but to go through the file may take five minutes - the key is I *know* where they are.

Following are some key points to keep in mind when deciding on homes for items:

1. HOW OFTEN IS IT USED? My coffee pot is on the kitchen counter and my slow cooker is in a closet in the basement. If you use an item a lot, then make sure it is handy.

2. WHERE DO YOU USE IT? Keep items where you use them. I know a lady who keeps her dental floss in her car and flosses when she is waiting for her children to come out of lessons or school.

3. WHEN DO YOU USE IT? Do you store things away during different seasons? In summer, the wading pool is out and the skis are in the top of the garage. In the winter, they switch locations.

4. WHO USES IT? If one member of the family uses something regularly, let them determine the best place for it. Just make sure they let everyone know!

5. MULTIPLE USES! If something is needed in numerous locations and is used by more than one family member, buy multiples. This especially applies to office supplies. If your teenager is reading along with you, this does not apply to phones or cars!

6. USE THE SPOT. Once you have figured out where things are going to go, you have to actually put them there. Back to those keys again - if I don't put them on the rack, I will need to look for them!

7. HOMELESS STUFF. Some things just don't have a logical home – especially if you are not sure what it is! Each family member will need some form of junk drawer or box.

Create an "*I don't know what to do with this*" Drawer or Box.

- Put in all the things that you just aren't sure what else to do with – coupons, loose screws, magazine articles, flyers, newsletters etc.

- Keep it out of sight.

- Go through this every four to six months and see if you can throw things away. If you still aren't sure, leave them there.

- Limit these boxes or drawers – one for the family and one per person is plenty.

- Know that it is going to be messy. Keep it closed and don't let it bother you.

For the next three days, keep these ideas at the top of your mind! When the mail comes in, deal with it immediately; when you find something lying around – decide if you really want it. Pay attention to what is working and what isn't. Hold a family meeting and do the activities. Pay attention to how you are using the space in your home right now. See if there is a lot of wasted or unused space. Think of ways to adjust things so you can use the new space. See if you can find the little changes that make the big differences!

Organizing tips from Moms

Put things back when you are done with them. *Karen*

Put all possible tax receipts in one folder as you receive them. *Mom*

Put the keys in the same spot every time! *Susan*

Simplify – if you don't use it for over a year, get rid of it. *Summer*

Put things in their appropriate place. *Laura*

Keep plastic bags in the car so when you are at a red light or waiting for someone you can give the car a quick tidy. Use one bag for garbage and one for things to take back into the house. *Natalie*

Get rid of unnecessary items so you are not cluttering up your house (or your brain) with them. *Mom*

Create a family activity binder to keep schedules, newsletters, calendars, etc in. *Mom*

Get rid of junk mail as soon as it comes into your house. Write down the important things and dates from newsletters, church bulletins, etc in your day timer and then get rid of them. *Patrice*

REALISTIC EXPECTATIONS

As one Mother surveyed said, *"A clean house is not the end all… there are more important things in life. People come to visit me not the house."*

When we have a family, we have stuff. There is just no way we can get around that fact. We have to work together as a family to stay in control of our stuff. By using some of the advice in this chapter, along with the time suggestions in the previous chapter, you should be well on your way to improving your Mom Managing skill set. These lists and ideas are by no means complete. Once you have discovered your personal style of time management and organization, look for materials suited to you for more information.

With these new skills as well as taking care of yourself you will find your life runs very smoothly (most of the time).

FINAL THOUGHTS

As we complete the Mom Management journey, I congratulate you on taking the time to find the *"Me in Mommeee!"* I do not need to tell you the importance of treating yourself well; you have now had the chance to live it and know the differences it makes.

Even as you finish the book, the journey itself will continue. As you move through the many stages of motherhood, you will experience many different challenges. Your **Life Map** will change many times. You will accomplish many of your goals and add new ones. You will find new passions and leave old ones behind. Your dreams will change. The one thing that won't change is your need to care for yourself.

At times, you will find that everything feels together and life is flowing smoothly. At others times you may experience bumps in the road. The activities in this book are meant to be re-done. They can be repeated in whole or in portions. They can be done yearly or as you feel the need. They are also intended to be shared with others.

As I have shared my experiences in *Mom Management* with you, I ask you to share your experiences with others. Share this book with your family, mothers you know and share with me your experiences in *Mom Management.*

165

Mom Management

I close with some of your thoughts on the meaning of *Mom Management*:

I think of mothers who are looking for ways to juggle their lives - as a wife, mom, career person, caregiver, woman and loving human being. When I hear the management part, it makes me de-personalize the role I have and allows me to think of real practical, applicable things that a mom can do to help herself, her life and commitments without losing sight of who she is - a real person - with feelings and a heart of gold!

I think of how to juggle time between all of your children, your husband, your daily housework, time to yourself, work, bills, and money. It is a very difficult task.

It is how a mom manages her time. The management skills she uses to get through the day and still have time for herself.

Mom Management is the ability to effectively coordinate and efficiently operate the multiple Hats of Mom.

It is Mom taking care of her life, and the life of her family - everything together, but also separately.

Mom-management is the process of taking care of your family, your home, your marriage, your commitments, your friendships, and your career while still remembering and actively nurturing your ideals. Mom-management is a juggling act; knowing that the law of gravity says only ONE ball can be at the top at any given moment. It's your job to decide WHICH ball is going to be up there!

What does Mom Management mean to you?

I look forward to hearing from you!

Tracy Lyn Moland

Tracy Lyn Moland

ACTIVITIES

Keep track of the activities on this worksheet. Write notes and dates in the spaces to remember which exercises you have completed and which ones you still need to do. Consider re-doing some of them as you enter different stages of Motherhood or to evaluate how much you have changed since you originally completed them.

Remember you don't have to do them all. Only do what appeals to you and what you have time for!

Chapter One   Date

Notes:

❏ List your dreams   _____
❏ What if Dreams?   _____
❏ Compare your lists.   _____
❏ Compare your lists to your life   _____
❏ Create a Collage   _____
❏ Prioritize your dreams   _____
❏ Pick your top five dreams   _____

Chapter Two   **Date**

Notes:

❏ Create Activity Storm for your dreams   _____

❏ Prioritize the activities   _____

❏ Commit to Three Activities   _____

Chapter Three   **Date**

Notes:

❏ Pre-determined goals   _____

❏ Am I setting goals?   _____

❏ Create a *Life Map*   _____

Chapter Four   **Date**

Notes:

❑ List the roles you assume   _____

❑ Divide your roles   _____

❑ Evaluate your roles   _____

❑ Ask yourself key questions   _____

❑ Focus upon your roles   _____

Chapter Five   **Date**

Notes:

❑ Pre-determined goals   _____

❑ Decision-making   _____

❑ Procrastination   _____

❑ Disorganization   _____

❑ Review your *Life Map*   _____

❑ Doing too much   _____

❑ People   _____

❑ Hidden Time   _____

❑ Questions to help prevent wasting time   _____

Chapter Six   **Date**

Notes:

❏ Getting Started   _____

❏ Your Commitment   _____

Chapter Seven   **Date**

Notes:

Chapter Eight   **Date**

Notes:

❏ Pressure Points   _____

❏ Downtime   _____

❏ Reminders   _____

❏ Understand Why   _____

❏ Identify Priorities   _____

Chapter Nine   Date

Notes:

❏ What works and what doesn't   _____

❏ Choose the right tool   _____

❏ To Do lists   _____

❏ Review To Do list   _____

❏ Prioritize your list   _____

Chapter Ten   Date

Notes:

❏ Breaking Point   _____

❏ Things that matter   _____

❏ To organize or not   _____

❏ What works for you   _____

❏ Apply what works   _____

Bibliography/Recommended Readings

Motherhood

Hidden Messages: What Our Words and Actions Are Really Telling Our Children by Elizabeth Pantley and William Sears, Contemporary Books, 2000

The Mom Book by Stacey DeBroff, Free Press, 2002

Misconceptions: Truth, Lies, and the Unexpected on the Journey to Motherhood by Naomi Wolf, Doubleday, 2001

Sanity Savers, The Canadian Working Woman's Guide to Having it All by Ann Douglas. McGraw-Hill, 1999

Planners/Planning Tools

More Time Moms Family Organizer –More Time Moms creates effective tools to make your life easier so you can spend more time with your family. *www.moretimemoms.com*

The Road to Excellence Daily Planner, The only personal planner that helps you keep track of your goals, your personal affirmations, and your life! www.jennyhoops.com

Business/Entrepreneurs

Eveolution, Faith Popcorn and Lys Marigold, Hyperion, 2000/2001

Mompreneurs®: A Mother's Practical Step by Step Guide to Work at Home Success by Patricia Cobe and Ellen H. Parlapiano, Perigee, 2002

Mompreneurs® Online: Using the Internet to Build Work at Home Success by Patricia Cobe and Ellen H. Parlapiano, Perigee, 2001

Mom Management

Life Strategies

The Aladdin Factor by Jack Canfield and Mark Victor Hansen, Berkley Books, 1995

Any of the *Chicken Soup for Your Soul Books* by Jack Canfield and Mark Victor Hansen, Heath Communications,

The Family Manager's Series by Kathy Peel
Be Your Best: The Family Manager's Guide to Success by Kathy Peel, Ballantine Books, 2000
The Family Manager's Guide for Working Moms by Kathy Peel, Ballantine Books, 1997

It's Not About the Bike: My Journey Back to Life, by Lance Armstrong with Sally Jenkins, Berkley Books, 2001

Leslie Beck's Nutrition Guide for Women, Leslie Beck, Ph. D, Prentice Hall, 2001

Life Makeovers by Cheryl Richardson, Broadway Books, 2000

Life's on Fire; Cooking for the Rushed by Sandi Richard: Cooking for the Rushed, Inc. 2000

O, The Oprah Magazine, Hearst Communications, Inc.

The Power of Focus by Les Hewitt, Jack Canfield, and Mark Victor Hansen. Heath Communications, Inc. 2000

Power Sleep: The Revolutionary Program That Prepares Your Mind for Peak Performance, James B. Maas, 1999, HarperCollins

Simple Abundance by Sarah Ban Breathnach, Warner Books, 1995

The Wealthy Barber, David Chilton, Stoddart, 1996

Until Today! Daily Devotions for Spiritual Growth and Peace of Mind by Iyanla Vanzant, Fireside, 2000

Time/Organization

The Complete Idiot's Guide to Managing Your Time (2nd Edition) by Jeffrey P. Davidson, Jeff Davidson, and Bob Losure, MacMillan, 1999

First Things First, by Stephen R. Covey, A. Roger Merrill, and Rebecca R. Merrill, Simon & Schuster, 1994.

How to Get Control of Your Time and Your Life by Alan Lakein. Signet, 1973.

The Procrastinator's Handbook, Mastering the Art of Doing It Now, by Rita Emmett, 2000, Doubleday Canada, a division of Random House of Canada Limited

Stephanie Winston's Best Organizing Tips by Stephanie Winston, Simon and Schuster, 1995

Time Management from the Inside Out by Julie Morgenstern. Henry Holt, 2000.

Take Time for Your Life by Cheryl Richardson. Random House, 1999.

You Can Find More Time for Yourself Everyday by Stephanie Culp, Betterway Books, 1994

Websites for Mothers

www.iVillage.com - an online community for women.

www.BizyMoms.com - Who Says We Can't Have it All? Be a Work at Home Mom

www.BlueSuitMom.com - Tips and advice for working moms.

www.CanadianParents.com - Canada's Parenting Website

www.Chatelaine.com - Chatelaine empowers Canada's busiest women to create the lives they want.

www.GoMomInc.com - The GO MOM! Planner is an ultimate catchall day planner for everything that is family.

www.MochaSofa.ca – Women Connecting for Solutions

www.MomsNetwork.com - Connecting at Home

www.MomZone.com - The Search Engine for Moms

www.mops.com - Mothers of Preschoolers – Because Mothering Matters

www.MyMommyBiz.com - For Work-At-Home-Moms

www.MyWoman2Woman.com – Bringing Women, Family and Business Together

www.Oprah.com - Live Your Best Life

www.oxygen.com - Oxygen Media is an integrated media brand that combines the best qualities of cable television and the Internet to serve women.

www.paguide.com - Canada's Physical Activity Guide

www.thebusywoman.com - The Busy Woman's Daily Planner's

www.TotalHome.ca - An online magazine for women and their families

www.WorkoutsForYou.com - an online personal training company that specializes in Mothers.

Give the Gift of Mom Management!

Wouldn't a Mother you know benefit from reading *Mom Management*? It's the perfect gift for Mothers with children of all ages. Being a Mom is the best job in the world, but in order to be the best Mom in the world, we need learn to manage Mom before everybody else.

Visit **www.MomManagment.com** or Order here.

❑ Yes, I want _____ copies of *Mom Management* for $21.99 Canadian ($14.99 USD) each.

❑ Yes, Please send information on Tracy Lyn Moland's presentations and workshops.

Include $4.95 shipping and handling for 1-5 books, $9.95 for 5-10 books - mailed to the same address. (Discounts available for larger orders, call 403-226-8798 for further details). Canadian citizens include 7% GST ($1.54 per book).

Payment must accompany all orders. Allow 3 weeks for delivery.

My check or money order for $_____ is enclosed.

Please charge my: ❑Visa   ❑MasterCard

Name_____

Address_____

City/Province/Postal Code _____

Phone_____E-Mail_____

Card # _____

Expiry Date_____Signature_____

Make check payable and return to

The Gift of Time

Bay 15, 1435 – 40th Ave NECalgary, Alberta, Canada T2E 8N6

OR Fax to 403-313-9216

About the Author

Tracy Lyn Moland is a Mother, a wife, a daughter, a sister, a friend, an entrepreneur, an author, a professional speaker, a teacher, a volunteer, and most importantly, HERSELF. *Mom Management* is her journey of rediscovering her sense of self. Tracy Lyn has learned that by making sure to include "ME" on her list of life roles, her energy and ability to perform all her other roles has improved.

Tracy Lyn, her husband Patrick and their two children, Courtney-Lyn and Mats live in Calgary, Alberta, Canada.

Tracy Lyn is available to present to your group, association, or business. Presentations include:

Mom Management
- Managing Mom Before Everybody Else

How Many Pairs of Shoes Can You Wear at Once?
- Balancing Life's Multiple Roles

One Hour a Day? Is it Possible?
- Time for You

Live Your Life Goals
- Create a *Life Map*

Time Tips
- Manage Your Time Before It Manages You

Is There a Counter in My Kitchen?
- Organizational Skills

Visit **www.MomManagement.com** *for booking information!*